SO GREAT SALVATION

by
R. G. FLEXON RICHARD GANT FLEXON
BORN 18 JUNE 1895, WILLIAMSTOWN, NEW JERSEY
DIED 19 APRIL 1982, AGE 86,
SALISBURY, MARYLAND.

How shall we escape, if we neglect so great salvation?
(Hebrews 2:3)

*Behold, now is the accepted time; behold, now is the
day of salvation.* (II Corinthians 6:2)

SCHMUL PUBLISHING CO.

SCHMUL'S WESLEYAN BOOK CLUB   SALEM, OHIO

Published by Schmul Publishing Co.
PO Box 716
Salem, Ohio USA

Printed in the United States of America

Printed by Old Paths Tract Society
RR2, Box 43
Shoals, Indiana 47581

ISBN 0-88019-407-3

Contents

Introduction

I SERVED IN AFRICA as a missionary and had R. G. Flexon tour with me to visit the mission stations there. After fifteen years I was asked to return to the States and serve as his assistant. When he became General Superintendent of the Pilgrim Holiness Church (now part of the Wesleyan Church) I served fifteen years as Secretary of World Missions. He was a very busy man and much in demand as missionary speaker and evangelist.

Dr. Flexon was one of the most powerful preachers and missionary leaders I have ever known. He was one of the greatest soulwinners, writers and campmeeting preachers of his time. He had an unusual anointing on him for giving altar calls. I have seen great numbers line his altars on the mission fields and in the homeland. It was always a joy to preach with him in missionary conventions, and to hear him preach.

I count it an honor to have known this great church leader. His books have been in demand for many years. I know you will enjoy his writings.

Hopefully, you will be inspired with a passion for souls as you read this book.

—ERMAL WILSON
Marion, Indiana

Preface
My Acquaintance and Years of Fellowship with Dr. R. G. Flexon as His Pastor for Seven Years and Our Friendship Over Many Years

WITH SOME RELUCTANCE AND hesitation, the following lines will be written with cautious delight and a measure of fear.

It is a great honor to be asked to write what will follow. I feel a sense of caution lest I might not get the facts as they were properly stated and a measure of fear, lest I might not do justice to this great man through what may be an overstatement or understatement in either case.

My comments will be limited to what I have learned about Dr. Flexon on a one-to-one relationship and what I have heard him preach or lecture. However, I will check certain resources to be sure my memory serves me correctly, or make quotation from his autobiography.

Brother Flexon was born in a Methodist Church parsonage. While still in his infant size bed, he was stricken with a deadly disease, which from every aspect would be fatal. An older sister who was deeply committed to God and in good health knelt by his bed and prayed earnestly that God would take the disease from him and place it on her, and that God would heal him of this deadly sickness so that he might live and preach the great truth of the saving grace of God. God answered her prayer and he was healed and his sister died with the same disease.

The above is not found in his biography. I questioned if I had remembered this correctly. I wanted to be sure. I asked a retired minister who knew Dr. Flexon very well He confirmed this as I have stated it. I still wanted at least one more assurance that I was correct. I asked a close friend who traveled with Dr. Flexon. He was a student at Bartlesville Wesleyan College, but at the time it was called Central Pilgrim College, where Brother Flexon was president. He had traveled with him with a quartet, over 100,000 miles, as they represented the college. This student confirmed the story and added that his sister died with the same disease. This I felt confirmed this report of the saving grace of God, and that Brother Flexon felt a great responsibility was placed upon him to preach the full gospel of the wonderful grace of God. This was a lifelong commitment, with a driving force to answer the prayer of a saintly sister who loved him and the salvation of souls more than her own life.

Brother Flexon was converted at the age of six. He soon began to sense that God had a work for him to do—to preach the unsearchable riches of Christ.

I do not know if this was his first sermon or not, but God anointed him with such power that the entire official church board was at the altar in the church whose pastor was his Methodist father. So one could see that his ministry began at a very early age and continued in one area or another until a few days before he died.

I do not remember any comments about Brother Flexon's pastoral work, however, according to his biography, he pastored several churches with god results and often under great hardship.

He was an evangelist in great demand while he was still very young. Evangelists, in those days, were expected to forsake all and give their full time regardless of their families or income. Brother Flexon said that he was often away from home and family for up to six months at a time.

I have heard him say that he had never selected his calls by going to a larger church and put off going to the smaller ones, but he scheduled them I the order they were received.

During his early years, finances were not easy to come by. I have heard him mention some of these instances while preaching, such as looking over the schoolyard trying to find a pencil in order to write his exam or report or whatever. Sometimes it was days without enough money to buy a two-cent stamp, and money for other necessities.

Brother Flexon was District Superintendent at different times in his many ministerial duties. He worked with a driving force and he expected the pastor to do the same, to which I agree. This did not make him popular. Few pastors have this inner spiritual drive and they uncomfortable around those who do.

Brother Flexon had a positive and intellectual method of preaching. In order to preach forcefully and effectively, in his words, one must "first enlighten the mind, second, move the emotions and third, persuade the will." He often remarked, "People do not act according to knowledge, but according to the way they feel." Many great preachers could enlighten the mind and move on people's emotions and yet be very weak in persuading the will—getting people so moved upon that they would respond to the call to be saved or sanctified. Often when preaching in a camp, convention, or wherever, when his co-worker was through with his message, he would ask Brother Flexon to give the invitation. He had a God-given gift to persuade people to be reconciled to God. I have seen him line the altar—of course, with God's help—after another powerful preacher could not get one seeker. He would be the first to give the speaker the credit for laying the groundwork for the altar call—enlightening the mind and stirring the emotions, which prepared the ground for him to persuade the will.

On different occasions he was asked to accept the presidency of Bible colleges. He was not a professional educator, but he knew how to get men around him who were. This is true of all great leaders, regardless of the area. Brother Flexon was a leader not only as a district superintendent and college president, but also in getting people to follow a lifetime as full-time missionaries. For several years he was the assistant to the General Secretary of Foreign Missions, and later served for years as General Secretary of World Missions. When he was abroad and saw the need to open another field, he committed himself to do so, but often found the General Board was not in favor, not because they were against missions, but because the church was not supporting as they should. He finally got their approval with strict orders not to open another until finances were more available.

I have heard him say a number of times that if every member of the church would give the price of a postage stamp each day, that the missionary work would be doubled! *Oh, may God help us!*

The following subject I have discussed with Dr. Flexon on many occasions. I could write much of it from memory, but to do justice to Dr. Flexon, I felt it would be better to quote his own words from his biography, *In Christ Seeking the Lost.* I trust this will be acceptable.

When I was elected as General Superintendent, I found in my lap the great problem created in California by the uniting of El Monte School with the

Colorado School to form the Central Pilgrim College. The people of California were very unhappy, and it looked like we might have a split over it out there. I canceled all of my camp meetings for the summer and flew to El Monte and met the committee that had been set up out there to dispose of all detail matters concerning the moving of the school to Bartlesville. They were very unhappy about it and felt we should move the school back to El Monte. The one great obstacle in the way was that the General Conference had voted for all of our Zone schools to deed their properties to the Zone. This, California refused to do, and the General Conference had said they must or cease to be a Zone school. I talked for three days with the committee out there and told them I come to California to stay until the matter was settled. I would be at the home of the District Superintendent and at their service anytime they wished to consult me. They finally asked me to reconvene the California Conference to consider the matter. I did and permitted them to discuss it for a day, but we could not consider any other matter. When it came to a vote, the Conference voted against turning the property over to the Zone and closed the issue themselves, so the school was not reopened. I thought I might lose some friends because of my stand, but I have the best friends in that section of the church that I have on earth.

The two years that I was over the Educational Department of the church as General Superintendent, I worked hard to get some adjustments in that department. Brother Melvin Dieter and Russell Gunsalus stood by me, as well as Brother Abbott, but I was opposed in every move I made by others who had done a lot of talking; but when the chips were down, they would not stand up and be counted. We are today reaping in our schools and also churches what was sown then. Because of certain personal disappointments on crucial church issues, along with the great lack of pastors to man our churches, I stepped down from the General Superintendency voluntarily to accept the presidency of our college at Bartlesville, Oklahoma.

During my term as General Superintendent in my areas, the Central and Western, I had asked the superintendents to let me speak at their camps on church extension, and many of them consented. I was able to raise many thousands of dollars for that work and in the four years my areas organized twenty-six new churches and would have more, only I told them to stop as we did not have enough pastors coming from our schools to man them. This great need got on my heart, so when I was approached about taking the college at Bartlesville, I told the Board I would do so if they would vote to make it strictly a Ministerial and Missionary Training Center and forget their Liberal Arts as such. The Board voted to do so, therefore, I was caught and had to accept.

We moved to Bartlesville in August of that year, and I assumed the Office of President. It was a great change for me, and I had to study hard to get my feet down. The educators of our church said I could not build such a school, that there were not enough young men being called to the ministry to operate such a school. I felt differently about it. I immediately set up an internship for the young ministers in which they would have to serve six months of internship under some successful pastor. They were to preach twice a month, do pastoral calling and visit hospitals at the direction of the pastor, hold prayer meetings and sit on all Board meetings without voice or vote, and attend all weddings and funerals for observation.

This caught fire. The first year that I was with the college, we had 137 students. Ten of them were ministerial and missionary students. The second year, we had 140 students and fifty of them were ministerial students. We had found fifty young men who wanted that kind of training. They came from all over the church, from the Atlantic to the Pacific. The student body had grown so fast we could not care for them. I had gone out and covered the large Western area from Alabama to California and Oregon. I had visited 200 churches and camps in the second year, raising nearly $100,000 on the debt of the school to be paid in three years. The school was booming, and I felt it would be there for many years to come and could build a strong ministerial center. That was not to be.

We moved back to Indianapolis. The General Board knew that my moving back would take me off the General Board. The Board kindly voted to invite me to sit on the Board meetings until the next General Conference, and through the General Conference they gave me a beautiful citation for my thirty-four years of consecutive service on that Board.

I was soon booked up in evangelistic meetings. These are the best days of my evangelistic work.

Labors with God's Bible School

After retirement from the General Church, he accepted a call to go to God's Bible School and College as senior advisor and assistant to the \president. This he accepted and he accomplished much for the college. He represented God's Bible School in his revivals, traveled with the college choir, wrote letters to solicit funds and sought for instructors as needed for every area of education from high school through Bible school and college.

After Brother Flexon went to God's Bible School, he approached me, as directed by Dr. Samuel Deets, President of God's Bible School, to return to the school to accept the position as Academic Dean. This invitation I did not feel clear about accepting.

When preaching in a revival he often asked the people for names of those they were praying for so that he might join them in prayer and he, with the pastor, would call on the same to encourage them to come to their revival.

Brother Flexon was a man of great faith. Many of his great efforts in raising money are mentioned in his autobiography, therefore I will mention only one of his great experiences of faith and answered prayer.

There came one of the many times when a financial need was very small according to our present economy. He was desperately in need of five dollars, equal to possibly forty to fifty today. While in earnest prayer,, God told him to go to a certain address and he would receive the five dollars. He knew nothing of who lived there or about their spiritual relationship with God, but he felt sure the impression was from God. He located the street and house number and proceeded to go to the address. He walked up on the porch and knocked. A lady answered the door and he said to her, "My name is Flexon."

Without another word from either of them, the lady turned and left the door open and went away. In just a moment she returned with a five dollar bill in her hand and said, "While in prayer this morning, God told me a man by the name of Flexon would be here and to give him five dollars."

She handed it to him and he said to her, "This is what I came after." Not another word was spoken, and as she turned to close the door, he thanked her and walked away. This is just one of his great examples of faith in God who promised to supply all of his needs.

Another gift from God that Brother Flexon had was being a champion at raising money. He could enlighten people as to the need— missions, education, or whatever the righteous cause may be. Then he would stir their emotions with powerful illustrations, and then persuade them to obey God according to the need. No, not everyone would accept the challenge and give. This is true in every area of life. Possibly more people sin against God within their way of giving than any other way.

I was present to witness the following:

Among the many miracles which God performed in the interest of His school during my years of close relationship with it, there is one I shall never forget as long as I live. During the God's Bible School Campmeeting of 1978 we had to raise over $100,000 for operation deficits alone. God was helping in the offering and the response had been good for the crowds. The last Saturday morning of that camp Rev. Miller told me I would have to get him $49,000 to take care of our needs. I went to prayer about it. I began to pray for the full amount when the Lord whispered, "Pray for $40,000." I told the Lord Rev. Miller had said he needed $49,000. God again said, "Pray for $40,000." I spent most of the day praying for that amount.

As soon as I began to receive the offering two people raised their hands for a thousand dollars, and then four or five for a hundred each. I then dropped down to one hundred dollars. When I did, God came on the congregation and then they began to shout all over the tabernacle. Hundreds of dollars came rapidly. Both ends of the altar filled with seekers. But I did not stop taking an offering. Some of the saints came and prayed with those seekers. But I never stopped taking the offering. They all claimed to get through and went back to their seats. The saints were still shouting all over the tabernacle and giving. Again God took hold and the long altar filled with seekers from wall to wall. The front seats filled and some were in the second row of seats. I begged people to stop giving and come and pray with the seekers, but they kept on giving and shouting. I finally told them they must stop giving and come and pray with the seekers. At that time they did. God gave a wonderful altar service with good victory.

When the offering was counted that night there was exactly $40,000.00. The next day the other $9000 came easily. God can direct one in his prayer life if we live close enough to Him to hear Him speak.

In my ministry of the past seventy years I have seen some great outpourings of the Spirit of God. These were in great church revivals and a number of them in the 160 camps in this country where I served as the engaged evangelist.

I am writing this final chapter of my life story on Tuesday afternoon, June 9, 1981. I have just been through the greatest campmeeting I have ever been in during my seventy-nine years of living for God. I am referring to the 1981 Campmeeting at God's Bible School in Cincinnati. The camp started on Friday night, May 29th. I was unable to get there until Saturday afternoon. I was told by the President of the Bible School, Bence C. Miller, that I must raise $101,032 during the camp to renovate the Girl's Dormitory. The parapet wall was leaning too far out for safety, and unless we could get that amount of money to repair it, we would be unable to use it to house the girls during the next school year.

I have been the money raiser for the camp for the past eighteen years. So I started on it the first Saturday night. God helped me and that night we raised over $30,000.

The spirit of the camp was unusual right from the very first service. The preaching all during the camp by the evangelists—Ross Lee, Wingrove Taylor, J. W. Vess, Rex Bullock and Richard Beckham—was the type that blessed the saints and brought the sinner to conviction. The singing by the song evangelists—Rex Bullock and Richard Beckham—brought the glory down on the congregation about every time they sang. The singing by the two choirs, that of the High School and College, was the best that I have ever heard them sing, and the quartets and trios were just beyond description. I have never seen such freedom in the Holy Ghost any place on earth as we had in this camp. Time after time the long altar was filled from wall to wall with seekers and many times the front seats were filled with some real definite praying through to victory.

The greatest service I have ever witnessed on the God's Bible School campus was on the last Saturday afternoon. As I mentioned earlier, our goal had been set for $101,032 for the renovation of the Girl's Dormitory. We needed $40,000 more to reach that goal. As the money raiser I felt alone and solely responsible to reach that goal. The time had come for the offering so I just asked the ushers to pass the cups and receive it. When the offering had been received I told the congregation of about 1500 people the burden for reaching the goal was so heavy on me I felt I must leave the service and go find a place of prayer. With that I walked off the platform and went to my room to pray and wrestle with God. How long I prayed I do not know, but I do know that all of a sudden a sweet peace came to my soul and the rest of faith gripped me. I could pray no more. I just rested in the presence of God.

Soon there was a knock at my door and when I opened it there stood Rev. Glenn D. Black, the Executive Editor of *God's Revivalist*. He told me the goal of $40,000 had been met and that President Miller wanted me to come to the tabernacle at once. Brother Black took my arm and led me to the tabernacle platform amid such shouting I have never heard. I could do nothing but weep and praise God.

Here is what transpired while I prayed. Evangelist Ross Lee stood to preach after the special song. According to the tape taken of the service a man arose and said he was coming to join me in prayer. He did not come to my room to pray but went to his own room. I was glad he did not come to my room for when God gives me the rest of faith when I am wrestling with him over something special, I never want anyone around nor do I ever tell anyone I have prayed through on the matter. The secret is between me and my Divine Lover until He sees fit to give me the realization of faith. When that man said to the congregation that he was going to pray with me the service took an abrupt change. The people started to give and shout. Brother Lee had the spiritual discernment and saw that God had taken direct charge of the service, so instead of preaching his sermon, he gave himself to God as the human agent for Him to work through. Thank God for men who know how to discern the moods of the Spirit of God and let Him take and use them. They are willing to let their sermon waith or never preach. From that moment on such shouting and giving I have never heard or known. When they called for me to come the goal of $40,000 had been reached in answer to prayer and the willingness of Brother Lee to let God use him as a channel through with to run His power.

While I cannot, at eighty-five years of age, carry on for the school as I once did, I am still going back for their revivals twice a year, their Homecoming Day, their Missionary Convention, and always at campmeetings. My job at these is to raise the money for the school; act as Senior Advisor to the President, travel with the choir each spring on their tour; write for *God's Revivalist;* attend all board meetings; advise and counsel students and faculty members, and travel with a trio or quartet on weekends to represent the school. However, most of my work now is holding weekend meetings, writing and publishing books, and winning souls for God and eternity. (From R. G. Flexon, *In Christ Seeking the Lost,* God's Bible School. Used by permission.)

Dr. Flexon had a spirit-filled drive to fulfill the Great Commission of Jesus to take the gospel to the ends of the earth that lasted for a lifetime.

He worked and preached so hard his physical body was driven beyond its limits until his hand and head shook almost continually. One day during a time of fellowship with Dr. Paul W. Thomas, just after having visited Brother Flexon, I mentioned my concern for Brother Flexon. Brother Thomas said, "Neither God nor man expect him to work as hard as he does."

Dr. Flexon, on his last general conference report, stated that he had worked an average of thirteen hours a day during the last four years, for Christ, the church and lost souls. The deep commitment of his sister when he was a baby, as mentioned earlier, was a lifetime driving force in his spirit-filled life with God's help.

After he was no longer physically able to travel and do other things for the college, he was still busy in many areas.

Just a few weeks before he died, I knew his health was failing and I wanted to visit with him before he went to heaven. I arrived just before noon, and about the same time some letters were received, a box of several hundred he had written for God's Bible School. He had sent them there for GBS to print and return for him to sign and to be sent back to GBS to be mailed to promote the work of God through the college. This would take him several hours a day for several days in his weakened condition to get them all signed, and then return them to GBS.

Less than three months later, God moved him out of his physical old house which was no longer a desirable place to live, into the presence of his Lord, God and Savior, which he had served in continued fellowship from age six until he was eighty-six years old, when God said it was enough and called him to his eternal home.

At his funeral, his grandson said, "This is a great celebration." And why not? It was the day he had lived for. Amen!

—CHESTER WILKINS
Anderson, Indiana

Behold, now is the accepted time; behold, now is the day of salvation (II Corinthians 6:2).

1

Religion, Man's and God's

RELIGION IS ANY SYSTEM of worship practiced by men. Man will worship. It seems it is essential to his existence. No matter what kind of religion a man may have, it is usually the better part of his life; however, no man can rise above the object of his devotions.

Any religion that is worthy of the name should at least centralize human thought, harmonize human powers and subdue human passions. A religion of theory and not of practice is of little value. It is not the ideal that the world needs, but the real. Theory alone will never make any man like God. False religion may be the worship of man-made gods or the wrong worship of the true God. It is just as wrong to worship the true God in the wrong way as it is to worship an improper object.

Any religion that promises rewards in a life to come without demanding a right personal, family or communal relationship here is false. Any religion that can satisfy without making its adherents holy is false. Any religion which makes demands upon its votaries without empowering them to comply with those demands is not true religion. Almost any teaching worthy to be called a religion will have some good in it, but will it have saving virtue or enabling power?

Confucianism may have its beautiful theories relative to how a superior man should bear himself. Its ethics may be of the highest order, but does it give its devotees any power to live its precepts? Buddhism may set forth its theories of right feelings, right speech, right actions, right means of livelihood, right endeavor, and right thinking, but does it offer its followers any power to live its principles?

Would space permit, one might write of the sincere devotees of Mohammedanism—who could with profit be emulated in some respects, or of the strong theories of the Roman Catholics regarding the virgin birth of Jesus Christ, or of the aggressiveness of the Seventy-Day Adventists, or the lofty ideals of Christian Science, or of the good works of unregenerated evangelicals; but do any of these have within them saving virtue or enabling power?

Is it not all theory and human effort? In some instances they may lead one to a higher plane of morality; but is mere morality enough? Will it save the soul? If so, then wherein did the rich young ruler lack? Morality is located in outward conduct and man's effort, which can never save.

God's Religion

God's religion always develops from the center, man's from the circumference. True religion is true worship of the true and living God Who has said, "Thou shalt have no other gods before me." It is of divine origin and is given to man through divine revelation. It must necessarily be universal and adapted to the needs of the human race. It must be adequate for the national, family and individual needs of the human race. It must be imparted by another by faith, and it must center in God and it must be able to restore man to his original state of purity.

The Reason for True Religion

Natural religion can never satisfy the human heart. It can never lift man out of his fallen state. It can never remove the depravity from his nature. It takes a supernatural religion to do that, and only the acts of God are supernatural. The dead spirit of man can never be quickened by a man-made religion. It takes a spiritual religion to give spiritual life.

The Reality of True Religion

It may be a mystery, but it is not a myth. Man may not be able to see why his own efforts cannot merit salvation. That has been the great curse of all religion. It is the Babylonish idea of getting to heaven. It is true that "faith without works is dead." However, there is absolutely no virtue in works. No person can ever live good enough to go to heaven. All of man's righteousness is as filthy rags. After he has done all, he is to count himself as an unprofitable servant. Through the merits of the shed blood of Jesus Christ, and that alone, will anyone ever make it to heaven. The *why* of it and the *how* of it have both been unexplainable mysteries through the ages. Just why the blood of Jesus Christ alone can save, and the how of its application have been stumbling blocks to most unsaved men. Why a man's good works cannot save him and just how the infusion of the life of another can do it is hard to grasp. The new birth is a mystery, but, nevertheless, a reality. When God enters the soul, one may feel the lightning flashes run along the fibers of his spiritual being like electric fire, but he can never fully comprehend or explain it.

Riches of True Religion

Riches bring financial security to those who possess them. True religion has in it a plan whereby its possessor can be confirmed in a state of perfect security. Evidence and faith perpetuated will give such an experience. The natural condition of man is one of spiritual poverty. All of his human efforts to rise above that condition are vain. Only as he is enriched by the true riches of true religion will he succeed.

True religion is not limited to the present life. It makes investment safe for eternity. It calms the troubled spirit over diminishing earthly aspirations as it magnifies eternal anticipations. By it one is kept from under the shadows by being lifted above the clouds. It may make its possessor forget the sorrows and even the joys of the present, while he revels in the glories of the future. It brings a heavenly life to an earth dweller.

Recipients of True Religion

It is adapted only to the state and nature of human beings. Angels or demons cannot partake of it. It is commensurate with human problems. It has been revealed only to human beings. Angels desired to look into it but could not. Its reception is for creatures of this world only. Its recipients must acknowledge their poverty. They cannot buy it. It is free in its communication. They must acknowledge their helplessness, unworthiness and sinfulness. Their penitence must be sincere, and they must receive it by faith and faith alone.

2

Dangerous Half-Truths

JESUS SAID, "YE SHALL know the truth, and the truth shall make you free." There is much talk today about the four great freedoms: freedom of speech and of worship, freedom from want and from fear. That is ideal, but is it practical? It is to be hoped that it is, but one thing is sure and that is that the spiritual freedom which comes through the truth as it is in Christ Jesus always brings practical freedom. We need to realize, however, that it takes the whole truth to set one free; half-truths are dangerous. Let a person tell just a half-truth about anything, and immediately he is in bondage; a fear grips him; he wonders if the other half will ever be discovered. And if so, what will be the consequences when it is? There is only one way to keep freedom of conscience and a freedom from fear; and that is, to always deal in truth, the whole truth and nothing but the truth. It is the purpose of this consideration to point out the dangers of half-truths.

Believe and Be Saved

Someone may say, "That is not a half-truth; that is the whole truth." As used today, it is only a half-truth and a very dangerous one. The popular idea that all one must do to be born again is to accept the Lord Jesus Christ as his Savior is to wrest the Scriptures to the damnation of the listeners. Even at holiness altars there is much wrong instruction. Workers seem to be in such a hurry to rush the seekers through that they begin to insist upon the seekers believing before they are on believing grounds. Most of the promises of God are conditional, and faith to appropriate them cannot usually be made to function until those conditions have been met. This is particularly so relative to the promises of salvation.

When John the Baptist came preaching in the wilderness, he did not say, "All you need to do is to accept the Lord Jesus Christ, or believe and you are saved." No! He cried, "O generation of vipers, who hath warned you to flee from the wrath to come? Bring forth therefore fruits meet for repentance."

When Jesus opened his ministry, it was with, "Repent: for the kingdom of heaven is at hand." When Peter preached his memorable sermon on the Day of Pentecost, it was, "Repent." The entire tenor of the New Testament Scripture teaches that true repentance is the only ground on which faith for salvation can function. Repentance in itself is not enough; neither is so-called faith, which is possibly no more than a mental assent without repentance. It takes both, and the place and function of each should be clearly defined by every person who attempts to preach a saving gospel.

SEE P 44, "THE SCANDAL OF PRE-FORGIVENESS" RICHARD SHELLEY TAYLOR.

The holiness movement needs some preaching on repentance—that kind of repentance that springs from a godly sorrow for sin, that is accompanied by a broken and contrite spirit; that kind that makes men quit sin as soon as they begin to repent; that makes them confess to every man as far as they have wronged him; that causes a man to put his confession in the first person; that does not allow a man to make his confession to become wholly an explanation; that makes a man to be brutally honest in taking sides against himself; that makes him confess to his wife and children when he has wronged them; that makes him pay store bills, even though they are outlawed; that makes him make restitution to the person wronged, and not feel he has done his duty when he has placed a certain amount of money in the missionary offering or used it to pay off a debt on a church.

SEE P47, "THAT BURNING QUESTION OF FINAL PERSEVERANCE", HARRY EDWARD JESSOP.

SEE P34, "EVANGELISM" JAMES STEWART.

A restitution is not a restitution unless it is made to the person wronged. But someone says, "What if the person wronged is dead or cannot be found?" Then God will forgive. He never asks the impossible. One needs to be sure, however, that the party or parties in question are really dead or cannot be found. After this kind of repentance, then one's will can operate his faith and bring him to a realization of that promise, "If we confess our sins, he is faithful and just to forgive us our sins." 1 John 1:9

SEE P19, "GODLINESS" CATHERINE BOOTH. BUT P26 FOR RESTITUTION.

SEE P124, "THE MAN CHRIST, JESUS," G,T, BUSTIN,

Salvation by Works

No man can live good enough to merit salvation. Paul said, "For by grace are ye saved through faith; and that not of yourselves; it is the gift of God; not of works, lest any man should boast." All of our righteous-

SEE P40, "GOD'S INTEGRITY AND THE CROSS," RICHARD TAYLOR.

SEE P27, ON RESTITUTION, SEE P31, "SALVATION AND GLORY," WB GOD BEY.   SEE P. 105 "SONS OF THUNDER"   SEE P.77, "A RIGHT CONCEPTION OF SIN," 1ST EDITION TAYLOR

ness is as filthy rage. No flesh is justified by keeping of the law. Just as faith not founded on the groundwork of repentance will fade, so works without faith will fade. Paul says in Romans that if "Abraham were justified by works, he hath whereof to glory; but not before God." Again he said, "Now to him that worketh is the reward not reckoned of grace, but of debt." And again, "But that no man is justified by the law in the sight of God, it is evident: for, the just shall live by faith." "And the law is not of faith: but, the men that doeth them shall live in them." That is, a man who lives clean morally, upright in his dealings with others and complies with the letter of God's law will have his reward here.

But when it comes to the way of eternal salvation, human efforts—regardless of how good they may seem in the eyes of men—are as filthy rags in the sight of the God to whom man must give an account. He shall stand righteous before God who realizes that all mere human trying to be Christian utterly fails in the sight of God and who stops working to let God, by faith change him. "Therefore being justified by faith, we have peace with God through our Lord Jesus Christ." After one is saved by faith, then he is, as James suggests, to show his faith by his works.

License for Liberty

Often men confuse things. They confuse what they want with what they need. They confuse notion with conviction. They confuse purity with maturity, license with liberty. Many things are done under the name of liberty which should be branded "personal license."

Liberty is the power to do what is right for the common good. License permits one to do as he pleases, regardless of who must suffer. When one is being criticized or persecuted for his actions, he had better take stock and see if the criticism is just because he is going ahead and having his own way, regardless of the common good, or whether he is being persecuted for doing right. If it is the former, he had better beware. If it is the latter, he must go ahead and take the consequences.

Men to be Christians must do right, regardless of the stress, disappointment and suffering it causes—either to them or to others. Men who are Christians will never do just as they please, or contend for their own way where no principles are involved when they know the action is hurting another.

Kept for Keeping

Often one hears in a testimony the statement of praise for salvation that saves and keeps from sin. That it saves from sin is the whole truth; that it keeps from sin is only a half-truth. The writer has often felt that right at this point many go down. They seem to feel that once they are born again, there is nothing more for them to do. They leave it to God and their religion to keep them to the end. I know there are some statements of Scripture which, if taken alone, would imply as much. Peter speaks of those who are kept by the power of God, ready to be revealed at the last day. And Paul writes about God being able to keep that which was committed unto him. But John writes as though there is something for one to do himself if he is to have fellowship with God: "If we walk in the light, as he is in the light." The greatest pardon God can give and the deepest cleansing God can perfect will never hold good if one stops walking in the light. One must bring the bottom of his life up to the top of his light or break with God. Jude, after warning to beware of men who turn the grace of God into lasciviousness and remember what God did to angels which kept not their first estate, admonishes one to keep himself in the love of God.

Only as one does this can he expect mercy unto eternal life. Jude says that the way to keep oneself in the love of God is, first, to build oneself up in faith. Faith that is not fed or exercised will soon become impotent, atrophy and die. Work it, bear things, make it accomplish things, and it will grow. In keeping oneself in the love of God, he must also pray in the Holy Ghost. Do not just say prayers. When you pray, be sure you do pray. Do not give up until you are conscious you are in the Spirit. Another important matter in keeping one's salvation is to be on the job winning men for God. Few people ever backslide when they are doing all in their power to save others. These who wish to keep the victory must also stay away from worldliness, hating even the garments spotted by the flesh. If one does this, then he can cry with Jude, "Now unto him that is able to keep you from falling." One should keep himself in the grace of God through faith, prayer, and through service in which he is seeking the lost and keeping himself unspotted from the world. When this is done, God will hook all his power onto one and keep him from falling.

3

The Tragedies of Unbelief

IN THE REALM OF belief in the supernatural, humanity is divided into several classes. There are believers, doubters, half-believers, disbelievers, and unbelievers.

A believer is a person who accepts God for what he is, obeys the divine commands whether he understands them or not, and commits all to God, even when he cannot see the way. A doubter looks at God's character, ability and faithfulness in the light of his own and questions, but obeys what God says in hope that something may happen. A half-believer accepts only what his reason can fathom and rejects all else. A disbeliever is a materialist of the deepest die and discards everything outside of the material realm. An unbeliever is a person with plenty of faith, but that faith is misplaced. It is placed in something or someone other than God. Where faith is centered determines one's vision; for, in this case, seeing is not believing, but believing is seeing.

Some people have their faith centered in their nation, others in their position, some in their reputation, and some in their education; still others in their resources, their religion and their relations. There are people whose faith is centered in what their parents, or teachers, or preachers have taught them and would not change, regardless of what God says. One whose faith is centered in anything or anyone other than God is headed for tragedy.

The world considers that the present war with its tears, torn hearts, broken homes, debauched characters, crushed nations, and slain manhood on fields of blood is the greatest of all human tragedies. But with all the war brings, there are still greater disasters—the many tragedies of unbelief. Both profane and sacred history point out numerous horrible individual and national tragedies which have been caused by unbelief. To write of them all would fill a large volume. There is room for consideration of but few in this chapter.

The Tragedy of the Fall

Words are inadequate to portray a more charming picture than that which God's Word presents of man's beginning in Eden. Can the mind conceive of anything more lovely than the Genesis account of the beautiful garden with its smooth flowing Euphrates and its gushing Hiddekel? The grassy banks of those rivers were lined with trees heavily laden with imperishable fruit; and while the lion and the lamb played together in the shade, birds of every hue warbled their sweetest notes from every bough. Man was the divinely ordained ruler of all this and, untarnished by sin, moved about through the garden at will, knowing only the love and admiration of all God's creatures and the fellowship of God himself. What more could he wish? But man did wish more, obtained it and has since never been satisfied.

The first move toward the tragedy of man's first unbelief was a step too near forbidden territory. Had Eve not lingered so near that which was denied, human history might have been written very differently. To remain too close to or to step on forbidden territory will always lead toward tragedy. The next step was a longing after forbidden things. This always follows in that wake of too close proximity to that which is forbidden. The third step was listening to a forbidden suggestion. There is always disaster in the offing when one listens to or argues with the devil. The fourth motion was a look in the wrong direction and to the wrong person. Hitherto, her eyes were on God, and she was satisfied with what he permitted; her ears were open only to him. Then she looked to another for instruction. A final step was a loss of faith in the One and a placing of confidence in the other—that is to say, there was a transfer of faith and a misplacing of trust. Such a thing always adds up to unbelief in God which makes him out the liar. Can anything but calamity follow as an aftermath of such a condition?

True, it was Eve who took all of these steps first. But when she became aware of her condition, she was not satisfied to bear it alone, so she enticed her husband. Such is the way of wrongdoers. They are unwilling to suffer alone for their wrongs. Eve did evil after being deceived, but Adam walked into the trap with his eyes wide open. He deliberately took sides with the devil and devil-led humanity. As a result, tragedy has dogged the footsteps of his posterity ever since, and the end is not yet.

Why all of the tears; broken hearts; disrupted homes; warped, twisted and suffering bodies; deathbeds and funeral processions; wars and rumors of wars; hate and hell? Unbelief. So long as man persists in unbelief, the results will ever be the same.

The Tragedy of Kadesh Barnea

When Israel left the land of Egypt—a type of sin—God's purpose in bringing them out was the he might bring them into the land of Canaan. Instead, they chose a roundabout route with trouble every step of the way. The best way for any soul to go from regeneration to sanctification is always the shortest route he can find, and that should be traversed as quickly as possible.

Upon reaching Kadesh Barnea, they prepared to enter the land. To perfect such preparation, they chose a man from every tribe in Israel to go over and spy out the territory. That was good and legitimate strategy. Their one fault was to pick the wrong men. Their names should have revealed to Israel their characters and indicated they were not to be trusted. Smith's Bible Dictionary gives the meaning of their names as follows: Shammus—renowned; Shaphet—judge; Caleb—capable; Igal—God will avenge; Oshea or Joshua—salvation; Palti—one whom Jehovah delivers; Gaddiel and Gaddi—both meaning fortune of God; Ammiel—the people of God; Shethur and Nahbi—meaning hidden; Geuel—majesty of God.

The significance of the names as suggested by George D. Watson is interesting. His thought is about as follows: Shammua means *fame*. Here was a man seeking distinction and reputation. Shaphat means *criticism*. Here was a criticizer. Igal means *God will avenge*. Here was a man with the spirit of vengeance in his heart. Palti means *orthodox indifference*. Here was a man who knew the truth, but did not practice it. Gaddiel means *fortune from God*. Here was a man feeling he was one of God's pets; no matter what he did, God would bless him. Gaddi means *good luck*. Here was a man who left God out, but trusted to luck. What a following he has today! Ammiel means *we are the people of God*, or we are predestined to be on top, no matter what we do or how we live. This man's spiritual following today propagates a doctrine which is the curse of our age! Sethur means *mystery*. Here is a man feeling God's mysteries were always so deep that there was no use to try to understand his truth. Do not many people talk about the truth of holiness being too deep for them? Nabi means *to hide*. Here is a man with something hidden in his life. How large a following he has today! There are two lines of truth with which a preacher now can snow under most any congregation. One is secret prayer and the other restitution. So many people are professing holiness who do not have their restitutions made to date.

If these meanings be true, and if, as we are told, names in the Old Testament many times denoted character, then it is no wonder the spies came back with an evil report. When they returned with their report, the unbelievers were in the majority. They admitted that all God had said about the land was true, but said that they are not able to take it. They looked at God's ability through their own insignificance. If one looks at God through his own inferiority, it will always cause misgivings in God's superiority. In such light, one considers his power ideal but not practical in the face of obstacles. They said it was a good land, but the giants were so large that in their sight the Israelites were like grasshoppers. They left God out entirely—gross unbelief. Where was the God who worked miracles in Egypt? Where was the God who opened the Red Sea? Where was the God who overthrew Pharaoh and his host? He was dead, as far as they were concerned!

There was one bright picture in all this dark unbelief. Caleb, whose name meant *ability*, and Joshua, whose name meant *God's salvation*, came forward and said, "Let us go up at once and possess it, for we are well able to overcome it." God's salvation coupled on to man's ability can accomplish great things.

The people, however, believed the majority of the spies, and how their misplaced faith or unbelief took fire. All the preaching Joshua and Caleb could do was so much wasted effort. Unbelief conquered, and the Israelites took to the wilderness.

They refused to enter the land in God's way by faith, and later when they tried to enter it in their own way, they were repulsed. They settled down in a state of complaining. They had the form of godliness, but not the power. They wandered about in the wilderness with no city to dwell in, with no settled place. They were ever longing for Egypt. They blamed their leaders for their misery. They all died in unbelief. It took nearly one hundred funerals a day over a period of forty years to bury the holiness rejecters. More people died in this one tragedy of unbelief than have died in all the wars of the country since the United States has been a nation. The greatest tragedies of all time are those following in the wake of unbelief. One is horrified at the great number of murders, suicides and other crimes committed in this fair land. One stands aghast at the carnage of the present war and the vision of the future world, and too often laughs at the tragedies of unbelief. What moral insanity! How much of what the world suffers today may be the result of the unbelief in the church and her rejection of God's standard of holiness will never be revealed until the judgment, but this writer believes that a great share of it will be placed there.

The Tragedy of Calvary

The necessity for Calvary is the tragedy of all tragedies. The results of the fall of man and its devastating effects upon the human race, the world, God and government can never be told. Its climax came when Jesus was placed on the cross. Had it not been for the disaster of unbelief in Eden, the tragedy of Calvary would never have been necessary.

The demand for Calvary by the Jews when through the blindness of unbelief they cried out, "Let him be crucified," and, "Let his blood be upon us and our children" has brought tragedy to the Jewish people and through them to the world. Because they cried for his blood, the world is now crying for their blood. For demanding his destruction, the world is now demanding their destruction. Their rejection of him in unbelief drove them from their own land to the four corners of the earth. The fact they are out of their rightful place is the cause of much of the world's suffering today, and the world will continue to suffer until the Jew is back in his own land with faith in Jesus Christ and crying in penitence as they "look on him whom they have pierced."

Of all the signs pointing to his soon return, the greatest is the one brought forward in the question by Jesus when he said, "When I come, shall I find faith on the earth?" He does not ask, "Shall I find denominations existing when I come?" or "Shall I find preachers preaching?" or "Shall I find layman laboring for my cause?" but, "Shall I find faith?"

Faith is the scarcest article in the world today, and yet it is the one requisite for being ready when he comes. Not just faith in the history of his life, not just faith in him as a miracle worker, not just faith in him as an ideal—such faith never saves. What is needed is faith in him. Not just faith in his blood, or his Word, or his work, but in him. Such faith will change the heart, transform the nature, reform the activities and purify the heart, for "every man that has this hope in him purifieth himself, even as he is pure."

Without such faith one is living in unbelief, and such unbelief will result in the tragedy of being left when the trumpet sounds and of suffering the pains and pangs of the tribulation judgments. Mark exhorts to faith in God and only as one heeds this admonition is he lifted from the realm of unbelief, thus to escape the judgments of hell.

4

The Mastery of Sin

EVER SINCE THE TRAGEDY of Eden, the war of the ages has been with the sin question. Back and forth the battles have raged between God and the devil. It was through humanity that God will finally conquer sin and the devil. It was through the first Adam the war was started. It will be through the Second Adam that the war will be won and ended.

As far as God is concerned, the solution to the sin question has already been provided. It was decided in the council chambers of eternity and was finished on the hill Calvary. Why God should wait to strike the final blow and claim the victory of Calvary is his secret. The day that final victory will be claimed, angels or men do not know; but his Word declares it will certainly come. In the meantime, men battle on with sin. The Bible instructs him in the method of the struggle and furnishes him with the implements of warfare. How he follows the instructions and uses the implements determines which side he is on. In this chapter notice is given first to some of the methods men have invented to master sin and then to the methods God has said to use.

Physical Torture

History repeatedly tells of the tortures of the monastery in man's vain effort to deliver himself from sin. Missionaries are still telling of the tortures of the heathen in their search for peace—they speak of the long journeys, of the heathen measuring their bodies on the earth mile after mile and day after day in order to find soul rest. When idol temples, monasteries, convents, Protestant sanctuaries and all human hearts give up their secrets of hopeless struggle against sin, how appealing will be the facts!

Deceived Complacency

Those who come within this class have very little consciousness of sin. For many of them, nothing is wrong so long as they can do it and not be discovered. For others in this class, the laws of the country mean more than the laws of God. They can break the laws of God without breaking any of man. To some, the breaking of a social custom would be worse than to get drunk. For still others, nothing is wrong which they personally feel to be right, no matter what God's Book may have to say on the subject. Usually the method employed by most people in dealing with sin is to close their eyes to it and do nothing about it. They seem to have a belief that one must live in sin all of his life, that it is a part of life and those who profess to have gotten to the place where they live above it are not creatures of the world.

All human methods have failed and will fail, but God's methods are successful if man will but try them. Notice some of them.

Amputation

Jesus said in Matthew 5:30, "If thy right hand offend thee, cut it off." Amputate it. Here is a method which is drastic. There is no halfway business about it. It is not the method of those who would taper off a little at a time. Some would have one to smoke ten cigarettes today, nine tomorrow and eight the next day. There are those who would have one to drink a little less whiskey each day or to dress a little less modestly with each new dress purchased or to see one less movie a month. God's method is to quit it at once. Cut it off!

This rule applies not only to sins against others, or the low-down sins. It may be applied to things as useful to the natural man as the right hand and just as dear; but if it offends—that is, causes one to stumble—he had better cut it off. Anything in life that is making one less spiritual than he knows God wants him to be should stop at once. Do not question. Stop it. No matter how dear it is, or whether one can see any reason for giving it up or not, if it detracts from spiritual life, it is wrong.

Notice, it is something man must do. Do not ask God to do it. He commands that man do away with it himself. To play with it is to invite spiritual disaster and eternal damnation. Jesus implies as much in his statement when he said, "It is profitable for thee that one of thy members should perish, and not that thy whole body should be cast into hell." If companions hinder spiritual life, tell them so kindly, and then drop them at once. If one cannot work on Sunday and be spiritual, he should tell his employer. Even if the employer insists that one should work, it would be better to go hungry than disobey God. That is the stand Jesus took. Space prohibits more detail, but suffice it to say that one cannot afford to allow anything in thought, action, friendships, reading, recreation, dress, social activities or even the church to interfere with one's relationship with God. One must amputate any such hindrances at once or suffer spiritual poverty.

Crucifixion

The cutting off or amputation deals only with actual transgressions. Crucifixion deals primarily with the carnal nature, sometimes referred to as inbred sin, inborn sin, the sin principle or the Old Man.

Paul writes of this several times. To the Galatians he wrote: "But God forbid that I should glory, save in the cross of our Lord Jesus Christ, by whom the world is crucified unto me, and I unto the world" (Galatians 6:14). Here is the picture of a man on one side of the cross dying to the world and the world on the other side dying to man. To the Romans he wrote, "Knowing this, that our old man is crucified with him, that the body of sin might be destroyed, that henceforth we should not serve sin" (Romans 6:6). Here is the provision in the crucifixion of Christ for the destruction of the entire body of sin.

Again, to the Galatians, he wrote, "They that are Christ's have crucified the flesh (carnal nature) with the affection and lust" (Galatians 5:24). Here is in experience what Jesus provided for and is spoken of in Romans 6:6. Still on another occasion Paul wrote: "I am crucified with Christ: nevertheless I live; yet not I, but Christ liveth in me" (Galatians 2:20). Here is a crucified life. While amputation deals with externals, crucifixion goes deeper, dealing with the root of the trouble. It deals with what Paul so many times in the first few chapters of Romans calls *the sin*. Thirty-six different times he calls it *the sin* and says it must be crucified or destroyed (Romans 6:6); that man must be made free from it

(Romans 6:22); and where it once abounded, grace must much more exceedingly abound; and that righteousness of the law must be fulfilled in man (Romans 8:4). Thank God, one can have such an experience here and now if he will accept by faith what Jesus Christ made possible through his crucifixion: namely, the destruction of the body of the sin.

Mortification

There are only two places in the Word of God where this term is used. The first place is in Romans 8:13, "For if ye live after the flesh, ye shall die: but if ye through the spirit do mortify the deeds of the body, ye shall live." Here the Greek word is *thanatoo* and means "to put to death." The second place is in Colossians 3:5, "Mortify therefore your members which are upon the earth: fornication, uncleanness, inordinate affection, evil concupiscence, and covetousness, which is idolatry." Here the Greek word is *nekroo* and means "to deaden or subdue." Notice particularly the latter as a method of dealing with sin. Here Paul, writing of certain native tendencies, warns that they must be kept under or they will result in sin.

If people would always remember that the human nature is never changed when God sanctifies it, there would be less stumbling over holiness. There are some tendencies left in human nature after it is wholly sanctified which must be subdued or they will quickly lead into fornication and inordinate affection. Such tendencies are proper and right when they are held in subjection, but when they get out of bounds and get on forbidden territory, they will leave a trail of destruction and heartache. Such desires are, therefore, not to be trifled with. If one realizes that such desires are hindering his spiritual life, and especially if they are leading to forbidden territory, he had better take himself in hand and curb them at once.

Even with legitimate affections the devil too often finds a gateway that is not well guarded. Paul warns against inordinate affections and admonishes its mortification. In the realm of worldlings, this faculty has run to excess and is unchecked, leaving in its trail wrecked marriages, wrecked homes and wrecked lives. Too many times among professors of religion there is carelessness and looseness along this line.

Picture a preacher who is making a success in his ministry. He has talent and personality. He is constantly before the public. He has chosen a wife, a clean, pure, godly woman. She is a model in chastity, an excellent homemaker and a loving mother. However, she lacks talent for public service. All of her work is done behind the scenes. In his church there is a woman who has talent for public service. Anything she is called upon in the church to do, she seems to be able to do successfully. Because of her position, the preacher is often thrown into her presence. He is frequently compelled to seek her opinion on church matters. Such association seems necessary and legitimate. However, it may be placing both of them on dangerous ground.

Their affections are wide open territory in which the devil can work. He will not fail to take advantage of the situation. If the preacher is not on guard, the devil will present to his mind a comparison between the wife who is fulfilling her God-given place in the home and the woman who is accomplished in church work. If such a comparison is allowed an entrance into his mind and becomes harbored there, his downfall is almost certain. In such a debacle the world will soon behold a wrecked home, a ruined preacher and a disgraced church. Such a suggestion from the devil should be mortified at once. If it persists in coming to the fore, that preacher had better remove himself from the temptation at any cost if he wishes to preserve his character unsullied.

How appalling are the number of wrecks right here! They are not confined to just one class of people nor to certain vocations. They are found along every highway of life. Temptation is projected through a legitimate channel, the channel of affection. Christians are commanded to love one another and to be kindly affectioned one to another; but when affection begins to center on the wrong object or becomes inordinate, it is time to check up and beware.

5

The Wrath of God

O that they were wise, that they understood this, that they would consider their latter end! How should one chase a thousand, and two put ten thousand to flight, except their Rock had sold them, and the Lord had shut them up? For their rock is not as our Rock, even our enemies themselves being judges. For their vine is of the vine of Sodom, and of the fields of Gomorrah: their grapes are grapes of gall, their clusters are bitter: Their wine is the poison of dragons, and the cruel venom of asps. Is not this laid up in store with me, and sealed up among my treasures? To me belongeth vengeance, and recompense; their foot shall slide in due time: for the day of their calamity is at hand, and the things that shall come upon them make haste (Deuteronomy 32:29-35).

FOR A TEXT I would like to call your attention to the verse found in Job 36:18: "Because there is wrath, beware lest he take thee away with his stroke: then a great ransom cannot deliver thee."

Our subject is "The Wrath of God." Many preachers are preaching on the love of God and they make God look like some little sentimental toy that people can treat as they please and get by with it, but God has hung red lights and signals at every turn of the road to warn men and women of what it might mean to go on and treat God and Jesus as some people are treating him. He sent this message across the path of not one but many people to warn them of the consequences of rejecting Jesus Christ. One of the chief reason for writing the Word of God was to impenitent sinners of impending damnation.

We find the book that has been written for that purpose continually giving out statements of warning. "But if ye will not do so, behold, ye have sinned against the Lord: and be sure your sin will find you out" (Numbers 32:23). "And as it is appointed unto men once to die, but after this the judgment" (Hebrews 9:27). "I tell you, nay: but, except ye repent, ye shall all likewise perish" (Luke 13:5). "How shall we escape, if we neglect so great salvation" (Hebrews 2:3).

My subject is "The Wrath of God." In the first place notice the fact of God's wrath. "There is wrath." Men try to banish it from their minds. They are ready to talk on any other subject but the wrath of God, and when you approach that subject, their conversation is brought abruptly to an end. Many of them say they do not believe that God is a God of wrath, but say he is a God of love. Where do you get your information that God is a God of love? You do not find it in magazines and books. If you find it, you find it in this Book. "For God so loved the world, that he gave his only begotten Son, that whosoever believeth in him should not perish, but have everlasting life" (John 3:16). But the same book that teaches that he is a God of love teaches that he is a God of wrath.

Yes, but that is all Old Testament. In the New Testament he is represented as a God of love. "He that believeth on the Son hath everlasting life: and he that believeth not the Son shall not see life; but the wrath of God abideth on him" (John 3:38). That is in the same chapter and of the same writer as John 3:16. "For the wrath of God is revealed from heaven against all ungodliness and unrighteousness of men, who hold the truth in unrighteousness" (Romans 1:18). These are New Testament scriptures. "Let no man deceive you with vain words: for because of these things cometh the wrath of God upon the children of disobedience" (Ephesians 5:6). You do not have to go to the Old Testament to find that God punishes sin. You can find it in the New Testament.

In the next place, I would like to notice the extent of God's wrath. God's wrath is a divine attribute just as much as God's love is a divine attribute. God must punish sin. He either must punish it or be a party to it. Sin is a principle. You cannot punish the principle; therefore, you must punish those who accept and live by the principle. The wrath of God is God's love in reverse—going backwards. God either must punish the sinner for his evil or become a party to that evil, compromise with wickedness, and condone sin. He who says he loves purity and does not hate sin is a moral leper. Divine wrath is divine holiness in action against sin.

I wish you could get some of these statements. Roll them over in your mind and digest them and you will see that God is a God of wrath as well as a God of love. But some people say God loves every sinner and even if he would go to hell, God will still love him. That is not scriptural. The Book says, "The wicked shall not stand in his sight," and "Thou hatest all workers of iniquity." He loves you until you deliberately reject his Son and defy him and put him to open shame. Then his love goes in reverse and turns to hate. God is angry with the wicked every day. If you will study the Bible, from it you will find the wicked people are not the John Dillingers, but the people who sit in holiness revival meetings and holiness camp meetings and deliberately reject Jesus Christ and trample the light that God throws across their path. In passing, remember that God is angry with the wicked and Christ-rejecters every day, and the only reason he does not put him in hell before tomorrow morning is because he has mercy mixed with his wrath. When you leave this world, there will be no mercy mixed with wrath.

The wrath of God is manifest. In the verse in Romans: "The wrath of God is revealed from heaven." It is not an abstract quantity or a myth but an awful reality. God help us to not play with it! The wrath of God is revealed from your faith. Every man and every woman here who are possessing common sense and good reason will certainly acknowledge that God is a God of wrath, rightly so and should be; but when we set aside reason, we make him a little sentimental creature.

A Methodist preacher was holding a street meeting on the corner and was preaching on judgment and hell. A police officer stepped up and said, "We do not want that kind of preaching in this town, and we will not permit it on this street corner." The preacher said, "Why not?" He said, "Because we do not believe such doctrines as sin and hell."

The preacher said, "I will give you a little story. In our church we had a young lady of good character and a leader among the young people. A young man attended that church. He saw this young lady and wanted to keep company with her, but she rejected him because he was not saved. So he went to the altar and professed to get religion to get a girl. (But they will give you hell to live in after they get you, if that is all they go to the altar for.) They began to keep company. You remember that after they had kept company for some time, one morning that girls' body was found down here on a lonely road and she had been strangled to death. You will remember how that mother brooded over her death until tonight she is over in the insane asylum, and you were the one that arrested that young man. Do you mean that the law ought to let that young man go and not punish him for his deeds?" That officer said, "To hell with that, friend." The officer was the father of the girl and the husband of the mother whose daughter was slain. If that fellow should suffer for his deed here, then God ought to punish sinners for their sin and for rejecting Jesus Christ. He said he did not believe, but he did believe in it after all.

The wrath of God is revealed to our feelings. Nature and instinct are never wrong. When a man is lying on the rim of worlds and about to take his departure into another country, the wrath of God is revealed in that old Book. Go back to the time of the fall, and come clear on down and you will see the wrath of God in every dispensation. The people of this dispensation that can laugh and talk about God's judgments are going to feel the wrath of God down in the lake of fire. If God has punished sinners in the past, he will do it in the future.

Again, the wrath of God is revealed in God's dealings with individuals. Once in a while, it crops out.

I was the president of one of our District Bible schools for nine or ten years. We had in there a brilliant young fellow who finished his theology course, but he said, "I want to get more education. I will go to the University of Charlottesville." He was there just one year. He was to come to our Assembly that year and be ordained. When the Assembly met, we received a letter from him, saying, "I will not be there. I have left the Pilgrim Holiness Church. I am sorry I was ever identified with such a group as that. I am ashamed of it. I am sorry I ever preached that Jesus Christ, that bastard, was virgin born of God. I am sorry that I preached that the blood was efficacious to save sinners. It is no more than the blood of a calf. I am sorry that I ever preached the Bible was the Word of God. It is a nasty old book. I will not be there."

He went to his home for vacation. As he was leaving his mother's home that next fall for school, she stepped up with a little Testament and said, "Son, I wish you would take that and put it in your pocket. And when you go back to the university, read it and come back to mother's God."

He threw it on the table and said, "Mother, unless you promise me you will never speak to me about that nasty Christ, I will never enter your door again. Never speak to me again of him."

The mother said, "You can stay away or you can come home, but you will hear about Christ."

He picked up his suitcase, walked out, and said, "I will never be back." He took the train for Charlottesville, but he never arrived.

In a few hours, he was back in the home where he said he would never come. They carried him in a stretcher. He was badly crippled up. He said, "Mother, send to the university for my professor." When the professor came in, that young man arose and pointed his finger at him and said, "Sir, I entered your school professing to know God, but you taught me to laugh at God and call the Bible a nasty book, and made me laugh at religion and God. But I am dying now, and God is laughing at me."

You can laugh if you want to, but the Book declares there will come a time when God will laugh at your calamity. He will mock when your fear cometh.

God steps in sometimes in individual cases and lets his wrath flash out that people might know what he thinks of sin and disobedience to God. I walked to a church in Denton. A man pulled my coat and said, "I have something to tell you. I was brought up in one of the most godly homes in Denton. I trampled the prayers of Mother and Father under my feet. I have listened to the greatest preachers in America, but I refused to give me heart to God. Finally, I married a lady who had been to God's Bible School and returned home a backslider. We settled on a farm and thought we were doing fine. Three children were born to us, but God was left out.

"One day when my wife and I were in the garden working, we looked up and the house was all in flames. There were our three children in the upstairs windows and we reached to get them out, but the house collapsed, and the three children went down in the burning ashes. We could hear their screams, but we could not get them out. After the fire subsided, we got rakes and raked three little charred trunks. We put them on the grass in the front yard, and could not tell one from the other. But as we stood there and looked at them, God said, 'You can trample on prayers and reject God's messengers, but now let me see you go to hell over those three little charred trunks.' Right there I got right with God." But if he had listened to prayers and tears and sermons, God would not have had to speak in such thundering tones.

The wrath of God is revealed against sinners and those who play with God's eternal truth. The wrath of God is revealed at the cross of Calvary, when Jesus said, "Thy fierce wrath cometh over me and thy terrors have cut me off."

The greatness of the wrath of God! The wrath of man is great. He has played havoc with this world until homes have been wrecked and empires have fallen. Man's wrath is great. The wrath of the devil is greater than the wrath of man. When he goes down to the earth with his wrath stirred because he knows his time is short, I do not want to be here if God will furnish grace enough for me to get out. But God's wrath is greater than the wrath of man or of the devil.

What has the wrath of God done? Just read the Book and you will see some things that the wrath of God has done when it began to move.

I want to notice in the next place some facts about the wrath of God. I turn to Exodus 32:10. The wrath of God waxed hot against the people that have just been brought out of Egypt by miracle power, but it is not long after they are brought out of Egypt until they are back worshipping idols. His people were up and down in their profession of religion. If there is anything God hates, it is for people to profess religion tonight and be backslidden next week.

If you meant what you were doing when you hit the mourner's bench, you would not be backslidden in the next week. You do not have to backslide every two weeks if you settle with God. If there is anything God hates, it is with playing fast and loose with God. The reason you do not get through and stay through, you are not sincere in what you are doing. His wrath has rested upon the people that do it. Listen—John Dillinger is not the worst menace to society tonight. It is you, backslider, who once professed to know God, but now you are saying there is nothing in it and God is not able to keep me. God help us! One backslider can do more damage in damning souls than all the John Dillingers there are in the country. It is not a light thing to backslide. You get in the way and become a stumbling block to other folks who have their eyes on you and watch your profession.

The wrath of God waxes hot against those who are insincere and play fast and loose. The world today has left the Old Book out of their thinking and their lives and America is putting it out of her schools and pulpits. If God punished nations before when they did away with the Book, he will today.

"He treadeth the winepress of the fierceness and wrath of Almighty God" (Revelation 19:15). God's wrath will be fierce. When will that be? It will be in the tribulation. How fierce? It will be so fierce that when God gets in the winepress and begins to trample his enemies, the human blood will be a river sixty miles long and so deep it is up to the bridle of the horses—when God begins to punish all Gentiles for rejecting the blood of Jesus Christ. If you read Revelation 6:17, you will never stop a minute before you will get right with God and do it quickly. The wrath of God will be fierce against the blood rejecters of this dispensation.

"For the wrath is come upon them to the uttermost" (I Thessalonians 2:16). It is indescribable. The very attitude of God is incomprehensible. We cannot tell you just what the wrath of God will do. But in the next place, you say, "Who are the classes who are going to suffer? Who are the subjects of the wrath of God?" Galatians 3:1, they are sinners who are rejecting God, and backsliders who are playing with the call back home, and believers who sit around and refuse to go on to holiness. It is just as dangerous to refuse God in getting sanctified as it is to refuse God in getting justified. It will abide on the children of disobedience.

What are some of the instruments God is going to use to punish? There will be an eternal consciousness of God's antagonism. You will be conscious that God is your enemy and that God is fighting against you in the regions of the lost.

Second, a reflection of the injury you have inflicted on Jesus Christ by your rejection and blood trampling. Just what you make Jesus suffer by your rejection, you will have to suffer through all eternity, only intensified.

Third, it will be an eternal sense of physical pain. When the pains of hell begin to take hold of your system, you will feel pain. It will be the horrors of wicked society. I wish I could impress it on some of you young people. Think of spending your eternity with a crowd of immoral, lowdown, ungodly of this old earth. I do not want to do it.

6

Is There a Hell?

"And in hell he lift up his eyes" (Luke 16:23).

A FEW YEARS AGO I was in the Main Street railway station in Richmond, Virginia, reading one of Richmond's leading newspapers. I was perusing what was then known as the Business Man's Philosophy. That day a businessman had written the following. "It is distressing to me that I must spend eternity anywhere." I thought as I read that statement, "It may be distressing to you to know that, but it is certainly a fact."

Common sense should make any person ask for the facts in anything and especially in that which relates to his soul's eternal welfare. Although the facts may be appalling, if they are well-founded facts, man should want to know them. Just because one cannot reconcile the fact of hell with the fact of a God of love is no reason for him to discard the facts relative to hell if they are well-founded. So many times man in considering the future state considers desire rather than reason or the Word of God. Sometimes the reason men do not believe in hell is because of moral decay in their own lives.

In this message we are noticing three thoughts:
1. The fact of hell
2. The population of hell
3. The condition of hell

First, we notice the fact of hell.

First, man's free moral agency proves the fact of hell. A moral agent is one who is capable of committing moral actions. If he is responsible for his moral actions, then he must be responsible to someone. He cannot be responsible to other men only, for they are created creatures like himself. He cannot be responsible to angels, for they

are created creatures. There is only one to whom he can be responsible and that is the uncreated God Who created all things. When he
faces his Creator—which sometime he must—and gives an account
for his actions, he will no doubt receive merit for deciding for and
living by right principles. That being so, he will then in justice have
to be given demerit for choosing wrong principles and living by them.
If he receives as merit eternal heaven, then when he receives demerit, he must receive the opposite of heaven, which will be hell.

Second, the laws of correlation prove the fact of hell. Two oppo-
sites are essential to prove every whole truth. All principles of quality, character and state exist in doubles. It takes the existence of both
to prove the existence of either. It takes darkness to prove light. It
takes bitterness to prove sweetness. It takes sorrow to prove joy. On
the same basis of argument, it takes hell to prove heaven. If there is
no hell, there could not possibly be its opposite state, heaven.

Third, the justice of God proves the fact of hell. There are those
who tell us that the antediluvian sinners will eventually be taken to
the same heaven that Noah will go to; that the wicked Sodomites will
go to the same heaven with the Friend of God, Abraham; that the
impenitent thief will go to the same heaven with the penitent thief;
that Judas will go to the same heaven with Paul the Apostle. If that is
true, then there is no justice in God or his universe. God must either
punish sinners for their rebellion against his laws and reward those
who love and obey his laws, or he is untruthful and is unjust.

Fourth, the holiness of God proves the fact of hell. His holiness
gives him a sense of rightness. Suppose the legislative body of your
sovereign state were to pass a law that any man committing murder
should be fined ten dollars and turned loose, but a man stealing a loaf
of bread would be sent to the electric chair. At once you would declare your legislators had no sense of right or wrong. That would
certainly be so. But suppose God should permit his only begotten
Son to die alone on the cross of Calvary while he turns his back on
him and declares it must be for man could be saved in no other way,
and then forget all of that and take all men to heaven, even though
they had turned down his Son and his blood and had substituted their
own ways for the way of the cross. Do you think he would be a holy

God? I certainly would not want anything to do with such a God. If he would lie, his holiness would mean nothing to me.

Fifth, the mercy of God proves the fact of hell. There are multiplied millions of people on this earth who cannot stand it to be in a holiness meeting here for one hour and a half. In fact, the vast majority of them would not even think of attending a meeting which had holiness attached to it. If they do attend, they are glad when it is over and seldom ever come back. If they cannot stand a holiness meeting here which lasts only one hour and a half, how, my friend, will they ever be able to stand a holiness meeting that will be interminable? You may say they do not like the shouting here, for it makes them nervous. In heaven there will be shouting like the voice of many waters and it will be continued night and day. You may still contend that you will be changed then. There is only one thing that can change the carnal man so that he can enjoy holiness and holy fellowship and that is the blood of Christ and that must be applied to one's heart here to be effective. No, friend, any person taken to heaven without a change of heart and a change of nature would be looking for a place to get out in a very short time, and he would be the most miserable person in the universe until he did get out. It is not a change of place or environment that makes one happy and satisfied, but a change of heart. There is, therefore, nothing for God to do but to put in hell all those who prepare for such a place by rejecting his Son, or he would be an unmerciful God.

Sixth, the government of God proves the fact of hell. The principal reason for the death of Jesus Christ on the cross was to uphold the laws of God. If his law had not been upheld, there could be no salvation. His law had been broken and there must be satisfaction for that broken law or his government would fall. Jesus Christ was the only one whose substitution could satisfy the demands of the broken law. The law being satisfied, God could then offer to man, as a result of that, full salvation. Man is, therefore, now damned or saved by rejecting or accepting that substitute. If he accepts him and is accepted of him, he is saved. If he rejects him, he is rejected by him and is damned.

This must be so in order for God to maintain his government, and this he will do if he must lock every son and daughter of Adam's race in hell to do it. All men understand that lawbreakers must be separated from law-keepers in order to maintain government. Do away with such a practice and government could not be maintained. Do away with your courts, police, jails and other places and ways of punishing men for their crimes against the state, and you do away with the state. Do away with punishment of the sinner for his rebellion against God and his rejection of Jesus, the substitute, and for his breaking of the laws of God, and you do away with the government of God. It is either hell for the lawbreakers and heaven for the law-keepers, or there can be no future for the human race. Therefore, my friend, if there is no hell, there is no heaven and no future for anyone and no future for the government of God.

Seventh, it is proven by the Word of God. Jesus is the best authority on future and eternal verities the world has ever known. We find in Matthew alone he speaks of hell eight different times. "But I say unto you, That whosoever is angry with his brother without a cause shall be in danger of the judgment: and whosoever shall say to his brother, Raca, shall be in danger of the council: but whosoever shall say, Thou fool, shall be in danger of hell fire" (Matthew 5:22). "And if thy right eye offend thee, pluck it out, and cast it from thee: for it is profitable for thee that one of thy members should perish, and not that thy whole body should be cast into hell" (Matthew 5:29). "And fear not them which kill the body, but are not able to kill the soul: but rather fear him which is able to destroy both soul and body in hell" (Matthew 10:28). The above are a few of those eight places, but you will find him mentioning this place in Matthew 11:23; Matthew 16:18; Matthew 18:9; and Matthew 23:15; and in Matthew 23:33 we read, "Ye serpents, ye generation of vipers, how can ye escape the damnation of hell?"

David believed in it and in Psalm 9:17 declared: "The wicked shall be turned into hell, and all the nations that forget God." Isaiah 5:14 says, "Therefore hell hath enlarged herself." Moses believed in it and in Deuteronomy 32:22 said, "A fire . . . shall burn into the lowest hell." Job believed in it and in Job 26:6 we read, "Hell is naked before him." Samuel believed in it and in II Samuel 22:6 we read, "The sorrows of hell compass me about." Solomon believed in it and in

Proverbs 7:27, in writing about the harlot, said, "Her house is the way to hell, going down to the chambers of death." Peter believed in it and wrote II Peter 2:4, "For if God spared not the angels that sinned, but cast them down to hell, and delivered them into chains of darkness, to be reserved unto judgment." James believed in it and in writing about the tongue, said, "The tongue . . . is set on fire of hell" (James 3:6). John believed in it and wrote, "Death and hell were cast into the lake of fire" (Revelation 20:14).

There are those who say they believe in hell, but they believe it is the grave. If that were true, then God is certainly a nonessential being. He declares in Psalm 9:17 that the wicked shall be turned into hell with all nations that forget God. Here he is designating a certain class of people who are going to hell. If Jesus tarries a few more years, all who now live on this earth will be in the grave; but, thank God, we will not all be in hell. That being the case, the grave cannot possibly be the final abode of the damned. There must be a hell beyond the grave.

There are others who contend there is a hell, but all the hell there is is right here in this life. Suppose I should take a gun and kill my wife, and then in five minutes after I have killed her, I take my own life. Is all the punishment I will ever receive for my double murder to be inflicted on me in the five minutes between the time I murder my wife and the time I take my own life? That is an insult to my intelligence. If God does not punish me for my double murder more than that, then there is no justice in the universe. We are aware of the fact that there is hell among nations and in nations, in the home and in individual lives, but, my friend, that is not all the hell there is. Somewhere beyond the line of worlds there is waiting all impenitent sinners a fiery, burning hell of eternal damnation.

There are others who say they believe in hell, but they contend that it will eventually be emptied and that God will take all of its inhabitants to heaven. This is the teaching of Hell Redemption. They teach that after one has suffered in hell long enough to atone for his sins, deliverance will come and he will be taken to heaven. Such teaching transfers the power of the blood of Jesus Christ to the fires of hell. The Bible says, "Without the shedding of blood there is no remission for sin." If it takes the blood of Jesus here, it will take the blood of Jesus hereafter to save men from sin. Again it declares, "There is no other name given under heaven among men whereby men must be saved but the name of Jesus." If it takes the Name of Jesus here, it will take the Name of Jesus hereafter. The fires of hell can never atone for our sins.

There are still others who say they believe in hell but it is annihilation. When one goes to hell, he will burn up like a piece of wood and that will be the end of it. Others teach that the body will burn up as does a piece of wood, but the spirit will suffer on for eternity. It seems to this writer that both of these theories are wrong. First, there is no such thing as annihilation to anything in God's creation but a change by fire or decay. Second, it certainly seems that the punishment in hell should extend to the body with which the spirit has sinned or that punishment will be much lessened. Does it not seem that Jesus taught that both the soul and body would suffer in hell when he said, "Fear not him who is able to destroy the body, but rather fear him who is able to destroy both body and soul in hell."

Then, too, if all there is to hell is annihilation of both soul and body, why have a hell for those who are cremated in burning, flaming buildings or have their bodies cremated at death? Full punishment in hell would seem to call for both the soul and body to suffer together forever.

II. We are noticing next the population of hell. It will be without doubt a place of kindred spirits. I did not say a place of those who are kindred in action. I said a place of kindred spirits. God will judge by the desires and motives of our spirits as well as the actions of our bodies. There is an adage which says, "Birds of a feather flock together." Kindred spirits seem to find each other in this world, and certainly they will gravitate together in the life hereafter. That minister who denies the virgin birth, the blood of Jesus Christ as being efficacious for sin, and the resurrection of Christ has in him the same spirit as the drunkard and harlot of the gutter; and when they leave this world, they will both go to the same place. The Bible names the inhabitants of hell. It says "the fearful" will go there, that is those who fear man more than they fear God.

"The unbelieving." The greatest sin of man and the first sin is and was unbelief. The first step back to God is belief. "He that comes to God must believe that he is." "The abominable, the murderers, the sorcerers, the idolaters and all liars shall have their part in the lake which burneth with fire and brimstone." "All liars." The professional liars, the political liars, the ministerial liars, the church members who lie; all shall have their part in the lake of fire.

III. The condition of hell. It is a place of our own choosing. Men do not go to hell by God's decrees or God's predestination. They go there by their own choices. It is the slums of the universe. The slums of our great cities are horrible places to have to reside in. They house the poorest and, all too often, the worst of humanity.

One night I was going through the slums of a large city on legitimate business. As I walked down the street, I saw a group of men gathered around a street corner. As I came near, I noticed a young woman lying in the gutter, intoxicated. She was so drunk she could not walk. The men were making fun of her. God pity any man who will laugh at the downfall of any woman, and God doubly pity him if he has been the cause of it. As I pressed my way through the crowd of men to see if anything could be done to help the poor creature, a policeman came through the crowd from the other side. He said, "Men, what shall I do with her?" Their answer was to take her down the street and put her in the box stall in the livery stable with the goats. That police took hold of her and dragged her over the cobblestones two blocks and placed her in the stall with the goats. Some mother's girl had lost her way, and who cared? I was too busy that night to do anything about it. The next morning I went to that stable and found that woman lying in the filth of the box stall, her hair matted with her own vomit, the skin scratched from her face, and her clothing torn. What a sight for one of God's creatures.

You may say that is not your crowd and you would pull your skirts from such people. That may be so in this world, but in hell that will be a part of your companionship for all eternity. No wonder the Psalmist said, "Gather not my soul with sinners."

What is hell? It is God's insane asylum where he will put all morally insane people. I was holding a meeting in a southern city. The pastor of the church where the meeting was held asked if I would care to go through the State Mental Hospital. I told him I would. The arrangements were made. We went to the institution and met the superintendent. He asked which department we wished to see. I told him the disturbed ward. He said, "I would not guarantee your life if you go through there." I told him to take us wherever he chose. He took us to the women's ward. The doors were all unlocked and the women were allowed to come into the corridor. There were old women and there were some in their teens. As we walked down the corridor, they could follow us. Some of them would be pulling at our clothes, others would pull at our hair, still others would rub their fingers over our faces and glare into our eyes with a laugh that would send cold chills over us.

When we had come to the end of the corridor, I told the superintendent I had seen enough. As he was leading us out, he took us past the hopeless ward. As we passed, a woman was on a window ledge screaming, *"Let me out of here. Let me out of here."* The superintendent said, "Hurry, men, or we will have a riot I cannot quell." He took us to his office and then he returned to take care of the woman. As I walked from that institution that day, I bowed my head and said, "Lord, if you will furnish the grace and hell is anything like this, I will never go there."

I was in a meeting in the east. I was preaching on hell. A young lady about twenty-three years of age jumped to her feet and cried, "Stop that." For a few seconds I stood speechless and then went on. She again jumped to her feet with the cry, "Stop that, I say, stop that." I stopped. I asked her what was the trouble. She came to the platform and said, "When I was a girl about sixteen years of age, my parents could not control me. They finally committed me to a mental institution, and I was there for eighteen months. If hell is anything like that, I do not want to go there. So please stop preaching and give an altar call so that I can find God." Needless to say, I gave the call and that woman found God. Better think, my friend, about where you are going to spend eternity.

What is hell? It is God's eternal hospital from which the sick never get well, but never die. I was visiting a friend in a hospital one day, and as I stood by his bed in the corner of a ward, a man in the far corner was dying. Two doctors and two nurses were by his bedside. All at once he cried, *"O God, kill me. O God, why don't you let me die?"* His screams were such that everyone on that ward stopped and even out over the campus—for it was summer and the windows were open and those outside could hear—stopped in their tracks. Finally, all moved on and then that unearthly cry, *"O God, kill me. O God, why don't you let me die?"* Everyone stopped again as if frozen in their tracks. All was silent in that corner and I walked over and asked a doctor how he was, and he replied, "He is dead." His suffering in this life was over. Death had brought release.

In hell, my friend, there is no death to bring release. In hell they are crying, *"O God, kill me. O God, let me die,"* but they will cry on forever for there is no death in hell to bring release from your suffering, but you suffer on and on and on. You cry, you groan, while the black ravens of despair take you from every stinking cave of hell crying, *forever and forever, forever and forever.*

What is hell? It is a place of no hope. In a mid-western state a young man was sentenced to solitary confinement in the penitentiary. As the door of his dark cell locked in back of him, the Chaplain of the institution took his station outside the door. As he paced back and forth by that door, he kept repeating to the young man, "Have courage, young man. The day will come when the door will swing open. The day will come when you will be free again." Such a condition can never be obtained in hell. When you are sentenced to solitary confinement in your dungeon of hell, there will be no chaplain there to cry, "Have courage. The door will open some day. You will be free again." No, my friend, there is no hope in hell. The door of that prison never swings open once it is shut upon you.

What is hell? It is a place when we are forever under the curse of God. At any cost let me have the approval of God, but never for anything earth may hold, however pleasant or dear, let me know the disfavor of God. I have often gone to the fields or the hillsides to pray in the early morning hours. As I have kneeled on the damp grass and seen the dewdrops sparkling on the grass, I have cried out, *"Blade of grass, you have the favor of God. Each night He waters you with a dew-drip and refreshes you with His moisture, although you will soon be cut down and perish." I then look beyond that blade of grass and behold the souls who have gone from my own meetings and been lost as they cry in hell. No water in hell.* My friend, you are choosing between God's favor and God's curse by rejecting Jesus Christ.

I was holding a revival in a southern town. The pastor asked me if I would go to the hospital with him to see one of his parishioners. We had visited with that person and were leaving the hospital ward when a person pointed to a bed around which they had drawn curtains, saying, "There is someone behind those curtains who needs you." As I walked behind the curtain, there on the bed was a man who a few days before was in my meeting. He was under conviction but would not yield. In despondency he had tried to take his life by slashing his throat. His throat was now taped together. His eyes are set and glossy. His lips are swollen and parched. His tongue is protruding on those swollen lips. A nurse is holding on to an arm, feeling of his pulse. With his other hand he is rubbing his fingers over the bed covering and putting them to his lips and tongue. I watched him for some time and then asked the nurse why he was doing that. She replied, *"He is begging for a drop of water."* I said, "Why not give him water? There is plenty of it." She replied, "If I did, he would choke to death; he cannot even swallow a drop of water." I rushed from behind those curtains in tears.

I walked down the corridor with bared head and weeping eyes. I left the hospital and stood on the street, weeping. What was I seeing? Not a man on a hospital bed begging for a drop of water, but souls who had gone from my meeting saying "no" to God and were now in hell crying as they moved their hands to their lips and then reached out for a drop of water, only to bring dry fingers back to parched, burning lips as they cried, *"Give me water,"* but, my friend, there is no water in hell.

7

Revival

ALL RELIGIOUS LEADERS AGREE that revival must come from God. However, God has limited himself by confining himself to the efforts and faith of man. There were never more people in the Christian denominations that at the present time. There was never more talk about religion, God, Jesus Christ, and the Bible than today. However, there seemingly was never more illiteracy about God, Jesus Christ, or salvation than today. In nearly every preaching service the writer has attended during the last year, the theme of the preacher has been revival. But all the talk about revivals does not seem to be producing them.

Wherein is our lack? To have revivals there are certain conditions which must be met. If these conditions are met, revivals will be the result. But if they are not met, all else the church or ministry may do will not bring a revival. We would like to notice some reasons why we may not be seeing revivals as we wish, and then give a scriptural formula that has and will release God in his efforts to give revivals.

First, self-opinions. There was a day in my lifetime when people went to church to learn more about God, his Word, and their obligation to him. Today one wonders just why people do go to Sunday School and church. Is it just loyalty to the church? Is it on the basis of duty? Is it just to please someone who has urged their attendance? Is it just to be counted? Or is it with a strong desire to meet God and hear from him? So many to whom we minister seem to have fixed opinions on truth which block God's truth from getting to them. They come and go from church with the same illiteracy about God, of salvation, and truth as though they had never been to church. Is that not because their opinions are fixed and their attitude toward the preacher is that whatever he says is just his opinion and they have a right to their own opinions relative to truth? Have we reached the day, as they had reached in the Old Testament, when every man feels his own way is right in his own eyes and that he has a right to interpret God's Word to fit his own life and that no matter how truth may be presented by the ministry, it no longer grips him?

Second, reservations with the Holy Ghost. Do not our programs sometimes circumscribe him? Have we not made our own plans and are unwilling for him to work unless he will work within our program? Do we not want him to have his way only if it coincides with ours? Do we not hold such limited views of what God's blessings might mean that it hinders him from operating as he desires? Charles G. Finney said, "Every real revival is attended with much emotion." We decry emotion. We fear it will get out of hand, and because of this we do not see any display of the unusual.

When the Holy Ghost took over on the Day of Pentecost, we do not read of any program, any great extensive musical entertainment before Peter's sermon, and no entertaining, catchy jokes to open the message. Just a few direct statements were used by the Holy Ghost to convict the listeners. The reason that the Holy Ghost could indict the truth to hearts on the Day of Pentecost was because the church, filled with the Holy Spirit, had created an atmosphere of faith in which he could work. How different preaching in an atmosphere of obedience and faith than trying to preach without it. Paul preached without it on Mars Hill and did not have a convert. Peter preached in it and men cried out, "What shall we do?"

What a responsibility the preacher and the church have together to not hinder him by limited views of his operation. Where the Spirit is free to work—all other conditions being met by the church—revivals will be the result.

Third, unwillingness to stand by truth. The only truth that the Holy Ghost sanctions and uses is scriptural truth. Scriptural truth always reveals man's need and Christ as the only one who can meet that need. The greatest soul winners in the ministry are those who first appeal to men's reason, second to his conscience, and third to his emotions. No man ever finds his way to Christ until he is convinced of the reasonableness of Christ's demands, of his own sinful condition and that his need can only be met in Jesus Christ. Scriptural truth may hurt before it heals. For Scripture is a two-edged sword. It may offend before it obtains results. It may plunge the listener into despair before it can bring him to a decision. It may make him fear hell before he will want heaven. It will uncover his sins that he might see his need of a Savior. Any church that will not stand by such preaching will never have revivals.

Fourth, the church will be brought to a test on obedience. If it is living behind light, it will have to bring the bottom of its life up to the top of its light or its prayers for revival will be hindered. If it is dry, it will need to tarry for a refreshing from God to open clogged channels. If there are divisions among the members that bring a rupture in fellowship, there will have to be confessions and righting of wrongs before the fire will fall. The mother of Jesus said, "Whatsoever he saith unto you, do it." The water could never have been turned into wine had they not filled the vessels with the water. The vessels in the home of the widow of the Old Testament could never have been filled with oil had not she obeyed the voice of God through the prophet. This truth is taught over and over again in Scripture, and the only truth that God will bless when he is obeyed is also as definitely taught.

I presume the revival under Hezekiah about which we read in II Chronicles 30 and 31 gives us as good a recipe for revival and the results of revival as any description we have in the Word of God. Notice, first, they could not have a revival because the priests had not sanctified themselves. What hindered then will hinder now. When they went down before the Lord and sanctified themselves, God began to move in their midst. Second, the people were not sanctified (verse 17). This is also one of the great hindrances to revivals in our day. A church filled with the Holy Spirit will have revivals. A church professing such an experience, but lacking it, will not have revivals. Notice, I did not say they will have a great number of seekers; but they will have revivals.

Third, the people were too busy to attend the called meeting. Before the revival could come, they had to put first things first and forget the material things of life and concentrate on the spiritual. Fourth, their families were not attending the house of God. How can we expect revivals when the children are not in the house of God but allowed to be in other places and engaging in questionable things? We cannot reach them unless we bring them to the place of truth. Fifth, some still had idols and the Lord would not bless until they had cleansed out the idols. Does he not demand the same today?

When the revival did come, it was so glorious they could not stop it, but had to let it run on another week. The preachers arose to bless the people, not to scold them, and there was so much money in the offering plates they had to build rooms on the house of God to hold the offerings. What a revival! Has God changed, or are we failing to meet his conditions of revival? All of our rationalizing will not excuse us. He is still the God of revival. He wants to give them today. Must he bypass the holiness people and use others to bring it on, or will we let him use us as channels to help?

8

Formula for Revival

LET US READ IN the Bible II Kings, the third chapter, beginning to read at the fourteenth verse:

> And Elijah said, "As the Lord of hosts liveth, before whom I stand, surely, were it not that I regard the presence of Jehoshaphat the king of Judah, I would not look toward thee, nor see thee. But now bring me a minstrel." And it came to pass, when the minstrel played, that the hand of the Lord came upon him. And he said, "Thus saith the Lord, 'Make this valley full of ditches.' For thus saith the Lord, 'Ye shall not see wind, neither shall ye see rain; yet that valley shall be filled with water, that ye may drink, both ye, and your cattle, and your beasts'. And this is but a light thing in the sight of the Lord: he will deliver the Moabites also into your hand. And ye shall smite every fenced city, and every choice city, and shall fell every good tree, and stop all wells of water, and mar every good piece of land with stones." And it came to pass in the morning, when the meat offering was offered, that, behold, there came water by the way of Edom, and the country was filled with water.

If you are familiar with this scripture, you know that it was relative to the time when Moab came down against Jehoram, who was the king of Israel, and refused to pay tribute. So the king of Israel called for Jehoshaphat, whose one great fault was getting mixed up with the world, said, "Is there not a prophet of God here that we may inquire?" And they replied that Elisha was there.

Whereupon he said, "Bring him, for he has the word of the Lord."

And so, when Elisha was brought, he told them that if it were not for the presence of Jehoshaphat that he would not even look towards the king of Israel; but he said, "If you want water, there's only one thing for you to do, and that is to go digging ditches. If you will dig the ditches, then I will see that they are filled with water."

We do not need just to have a great time feeding ourselves, although we want that. More than that, I would like to see a mighty outpouring of the Spirit of God. I would like to see something that is out of the ordinary—something that is supernatural—and if I see that, there is something that you and I are going to have to do.

Charles G. Finney said, "An old-fashioned revival is no more a miracle than is a good crop of corn." He further stated that if you want a good crop of corn, there are certain things you must do in order to have it. If you do your part, then God sends the sunshine, the rain, and you will have a corn crop. If we are going to have a mighty, old-fashioned revival, there is something we must do and it seems that thing is to dig some ditches. In a simple message I would like to point out some of the ditches that we may have to dig in order to have an old-fashioned revival.

The first thing I want to notice is the ditch of old-fashioned convictions. There is a lot of difference between notions and convictions. Beloved, notions you and I may have by the thousands today and throw them away tomorrow, and still keep the victory. But when we have convictions, they are the truths of God applied to our hearts by the Holy Ghost, and once conviction, always conviction. Once light, always light. If I would build again the things that once I destroyed, I make myself a transgressor. What was once right for me is still right for me. What was once wrong for me to do, it still is wrong for me to do.

God gave me some old-fashioned Bible convictions when I was first saved, and I have not been trying to get other people to live by my convictions, but I have been blessed by God for living by them myself and I do not feel inclined to give up the convictions that God once gave me. If I did, I would feel that I was a backslider and, after all, friend, it is not what we shout over in church that counts; it is what we stand for when we get back home after the service is finished that will really count for God and lost humanity. So the first ditch that we need to dig is the ditch of old-fashioned, God-given convictions.

The next ditch that we need to dig is the ditch of penitence. Beloved, it ought to be just as easy now to have to ask forgiveness of someone because we feel we have wronged them as it was the day God saved us. If we could have old-fashioned penitence until people today would straighten up as well as they did when they first were saved, we would see more old-fashioned revivals.

I was in a church just a few weeks ago where they had been having early morning prayer meeting for months from five o'clock until six o'clock in the morning. On that Sunday morning of that great revival as I was preaching on being filled with the Spirit, people arose and started for the altar. I kept right on preaching, and people got up and began to walk over to each other and confess and fix up and straighten up all wrongs. As they did, the Holy Ghost kept settling down on that meeting.

As I happened to be preaching for a few seconds on tithing, a trained nurse from the city hospital got out of her seat, lifted her arm with a wad of bills in her hand and threw the money over the pulpit into the hands of the pastor of the church. What was the matter? She had been living behind light and had not been paying her tithe and had some money in her hand that was rather warm and she wanted to get rid of it quickly. About that time God struck that place and that Sunday morning service over four hundred people bowed at the altar and sought God. All in one Sunday morning service! Why? Because some ˌ ɔple got the ditch of penitence dug and cleaned out.

We will also need to dig the ditch of old-fashioned forgiveness. If we can have more of the spirit of forgiveness around the country, we will have more old-fashioned revivals and more people coming to God. Down in Snow Camp, North Carolina, in a tent meeting one morning, a little woman was at the altar and she looked up in the face of the evangelist and said, "Evangelist, I don't believe what you said this morning."

He said, "What did I say that you don't believe?"

She said, "You made the statement that I would have to forgive everybody who had ever wronged me, whether they ask it or not, and I don't believe that."

He said, "Sister, that's the Book, and I stand back to back on the Book; but tell me your story."

She said, "Back in this tent there's a man who a few years ago came to my home, called my husband out on the front step and shot him, walked off, and left him dead. There is that man. They put him in the penitentiary for four months, but his money bought him out. He's sitting back there, free, today. Do you mean to tell me that I'll have to forgive that man for murdering my husband and the support of my children?"

It was a difficult thing to answer, but he replied, "Sister, do you want to ask God to put forgiveness in your heart for that man?"

She said, "No, but I will."

She dropped her head on the altar and soon she arose, went back to that man who was sitting with his wife and daughter, reached out her hand and he took it. She said, "Oh, Lord, if thou hast put forgiveness in my heart for this man, please make him go to the altar."

He stepped around her and went to the altar, and the wife followed him; then the daughter followed the mother, and that morning seventy people went to that altar and prayed through and found God. A little woman dug the ditch of old-fashioned forgiveness!

The next ditch that we need to dig is the ditch of prayer. Beloved, we will never have an old-fashioned outpouring unless we go on our knees, pray it down, and let God really come. In the eleventh chapter of Luke you will find a chapter on prayer. In the first place you will notice that there Jesus is giving us the plan of prayer. Then he is giving us the parable of prayer. Later he is giving us the promise of prayer, after which he is giving us the purpose of prayer. Still later he is giving us the realms of prayer, and, finally, he is giving us the laws of prayer. I shall only call your attention to the last three: namely, the purpose of prayer, the realms of prayer and the laws of prayer.

Notice, if you will, then, the purpose of prayer. The purpose of prayer is not for repairs, but for refreshing. Do you know that if some people would take their automobiles to the garage for a checkup more often, they would not have so many breakdowns on the highway? And if some folk would go to prayer for the purpose of refreshing more often, they would not have so many breakdowns in their spiritual life. There is one baptism with the Holy Spirit but, thank God, there are thousands of fresh anointings, and we ought to have a fresh anointing at least once every twenty-four hours.

Again, prayer is to put us in the place where we can really get in touch with God. There is a motto on the wall in many homes which reads thus: "Prayer Changes Things." But I have learned that prayer changes me towards things, whether it changes the things or not. There are some things that I have prayed about and asked God to change that he never alters; but, thank, God, when he does not change things, he gives me grace to endure them and to adjust to them. So prayer does not change things only, but it does positionize us.

I notice in the next place the realms of prayer. Now there are three great realms of prayer, and most of us never get beyond the first. The first one is the realm of communion—this is where you and I get in touch with God. This is the realm where the emotions are stirred and sometimes tears will come into our eyes and run down our faces. This is the realm where we feel the current moving on the mind and we know that we have made contact with divinity; and you and I have never prayed until we first have made that contact. Anything beyond that is multiplying words and phrases.

As far as I am concerned, if I wanted to telephone to my wife long-distance, the company would never charge me for that call until my wife greeted me on the other end of the line. But the minute she spoke on the other end of the line, they would charge me for the call, whether or not I ever said another word.

God does not charge us with prayers until he has answered on the other end of the line. But, thank God, when he speaks on the other end of the line, then, beloved, you are in the place where you can step out of the realm of communion and get over into the realm of petition and that is the realm where you can get your own personal needs supplied. You need not run around the country telling hard-luck stories, for you are in the realm in which you can talk to your Father about every need that you have. In Matthew, the sixth chapter, and the twenty-eighth verse it says: "Consider the lilies of the field, how they grow; they toil not, neither do they spin: and yet I say unto you, that even Solomon in all his glory was not arrayed like one of these."

For it is not so much, after all, the devil which keeps us from having the things we need; but rather it is the cares of life and the deceitfulness of riches that are hindering us from being spiritual and from being what God would have us to be, getting our prayers through and getting our needs supplied. I am glad that since I have gotten into the missionary work of our church—where I have to pray down thirty thousand dollars every month beyond what the church underwrites in order to keep the missionary work in operation—I understand this. That means a lot to put to prayer. I am glad that way back there in my early life I learned some lessons on prayer that stand me in good stead today.

I have previously related how my family turned me down and would not give me one cent to get to school or to pay my way, and I wanted to go because God wanted me to go. So one afternoon in prayer I pled for

God to supply money to get to school. I needed sixteen dollars to pay for my ticket, and I did not have one cent. While I was on my knees, the Lord said, "Will you be willing to go and order your ticket, although you don't have a cent to your name?"

I said, "Yes, Lord, I will."

I jumped on my bicycle and rode to the depot, ordered a ticket from New Jersey to North Carolina, and I did not have any money to pay for it. But the next day the Holy Ghost directed me to go over into the country about seven miles to a little Methodist church. I did not know that they were having a revival, but they were. The pastor asked me to come back the next night and preach for him, and some friends found it out and asked me to come for supper. So I went and after sitting down at the table and asking the blessing, I turned my plate over and there were three five-dollar bills under the plate, and I had not told a soul that I needed a thing. Time passed, and it was time for me to go and purchase my ticket. I had only fifteen dollars to get a sixteen-dollar ticket. I had a man to take me to the depot. He looked over and said, "Brother Flexon, the Holy Ghost is telling me that you need a dollar. Do you?"

I said, "If God is telling you that I do, I must need it." And he put his hand into his pocketbook and handed me the dollar. I had enough to buy my ticket and get to school. I have learned some lessons on prayer, have you?

I believe one of the greatest lessons I ever learned was while I was in Virginia on a pastorate. We were seven miles from the store, and I had to go there on business. There was a large river and a toll bridge to cross. I said, "Wife, do you have fifteen cents for the toll?"

She said, "I don't have a penny." I had no money, but I climbed into the buggy and started for town. I got within two hundred yards of the bridge and tied the horse to a tree by the side of the road and started walking toward the bridge. It took a nickel to get across and I did not have a penny. My head was down, and as I kept walking I asked God to furnish the nickel to get across. Just as I was about to step on the first plank of the bridge, I looked down—I will never forget that plank—and there was a nickel. I picked it up and went on across and paid my toll. Amen!

The Book says, "But my God shall supply all your need according to his riches in glory by Christ Jesus" (Philippians 4:19). Will you let me testify that while I have to pray in thirty thousand dollars a month to keep the missionary work going in our church, it has been years since I have ever asked God to supply my own personal needs?

People say, "How are they supplied?"

"But seek ye first the kingdom of God, and his righteousness; and all these things shall be added unto you" (Matthew 6:33).

Thank the Lord, if you will put God first, he will put you and me first and see that our needs are certainly supplied!

The next realm is the realm of intercession and that is the realm where you are not concerned about your personal needs. You are not concerned about whether or not you have meals to eat, whether your clothes are patched or new, whether you have a brand new automobile, but rather your concern is for a lost world that is going to hell without God. God can swing you out into the realm of intercession where he can put a whole family on your heart, a whole church on your heart, a whole community on your heart, and sometimes a whole nation on your heart. Make sure you will be true to him in prayer and not give up until he rolls the burden from your heart.

Sometimes when you are in that realm if you keep a diary, when you arise in the morning, you can write in your diary: "I spent all last night alone with God in prayer, not for my own soul's blessing, nor for repairs, but to pray over a lost world that is going to hell." Do you know what this world needs today? It is a ministry of intercession—intercessory prayer. We have great preachers; but, oh, I am praying that God will give us some great prayers around the holiness movement that will be intercessors and spend time alone with him.

I was in the Delanco, New Jersey, camp some years ago. I arose to preach on the last Sunday night, but I did not even get to take my text. People started to run to the altar. But just before I got up to preach, the president of the camp, Dr. Hamilton, had called on a medical doctor, Dr. Hodgin, to pray. He got down on his knees and said, "Lord, this meeting is thine . . .Amen!" Before the rest of us got down, he was up and was taking his seat. That is all the praying that we had in the meeting, but what an outpouring of the Spirit of God!

After the service I went to him and asked, "Dr. Hodgin, why didn't you pray when you were called out?"

He said, "Brother Flexon, I didn't have to pray in the service tonight. I spent all night last night in prayer alone for this meeting tonight, and just about the time that the sun was rising I prayed through, and so I did not have to pray anymore about it." Amen! If you and I get to the place where we do not stop until we have prayed the thing through and we have heard from heaven in the realm of intercessory prayer, we will see things come to pass.

Then, beloved, you will notice that prayer has law. Love has law, faith has law, and so does prayer have laws. Notice, if you will, some of the laws of prayer. The first law of prayer is the law of sincerity. "If I regard iniquity in my heart, the Lord will not hear me" (Psalm 66:18). There is no use to pray while you still have things covered up in your heart that you are unwilling to make right.

The next law is the law of unity with Christ. "If ye abide in me, and my words abide in you, ye shall ask what you will, and it shall be done unto you" (John. 15:7). Thank the Lord! The next law of prayer is the law of relationship. "If ye then being evil, know how to give good gifts to your children, how much more shall your Father which is in heaven give good things to them that ask him."

Moreover, there is the law of importunity. A man went to his friend in the middle of the night and asked for three loaves of bread.

His friend said, "Go home! I'm in bed with my children. I can't rise and give you."

The man never stopped. He said, "I want three loaves."

And he kept repeating that until the man got up and gave him three loaves. One statement that I heard Joseph Smith make is as follows: "When you start to pray for a thing, never stop until you get it." That has been my practice ever since. This demonstrates the law of importunity.

There is also the law of desire. God does not give us everything that we ask for, but he does give us what we desire; for prayer is not what we ask for with our lips, but it is the desire of our hearts.

And then there is, furthermore, the law of preparation. Beyond that, there is the law of cooperation with God. Sometimes, when we ask God to do a thing, we have to be willing to do it ourselves if we can before God will ever answer our prayers. I will never forget when a few years ago in missionary work, we needed six automobiles for the field. One morning in the camp meeting at Allentown, Pennsylvania, about sunrise I was on my knees, saying, "Oh, God, please make somebody come on these grounds today that will give an automobile for the foreign field."

The Holy Ghost said, "Why don't you give one?" I tried to pray around it and under it and over it. I did not have the money with which to buy a car.

I said, "Oh, God, please make somebody come on this campground today that will give an automobile for the mission field."

Again the Holy Ghost said, "Why don't you give one?"

He kept it up until finally I looked up and said, "Lord, I'll give one, though I don't have anything with which to buy a car." The burden rolled from my heart. I walked out of the room and as I crossed the campus, there was the man from whom I had purchased my car.

I went over and said, "Let's take a ride." I talked to him about what God had told me concerning the car.

When we returned to the campground, he said, "Brother Flexon, you're sure that God wants you to buy this car?"

I replied, "Yes, I am."

He said, "When you are ready for your car, come over to the garage and pick out any car you want and the company will give it to you." Praise the Lord! The next year he gave me another one, and the next year he gave me another one, and the next year he gave me two; and every year since he has been giving me a car for mission fields.

When you ask God to do a thing, he may want you to help out. If I had said, "Lord, I can't do it, for I don't have a cent with which to buy a car," I would have stopped the whole car procession. Because I was willing to do it when I had nothing with which to buy it, the cars are still coming. Do you know what I am talking about? Have you ever really prayed for anything and gotten answers to your prayers?

The seventh ditch we need to dig is the ditch of love for souls. When God saved me, I was standing on the platform on a Sunday afternoon beside my father as he preached in a mission hall. He gave the altar call, and I stood beside him. There was a big six-footer back there at the back bench, and he was holding his songbook and trying to sing. The Holy Ghost said to me, a child of six years, "Go back and invite that man to the altar."

I left the platform and walked back and looked up into the face of that big six-footer and said, "Mister, don't you want to come to the altar and give your heart to God?" He just lifted the book a little higher and ignored me, but I was not to be outdone like that.

I climbed on the bench alongside him, put my arms around his neck and got my mouth as close to his ear as I could possibly get it and said, "Mister, don't you want to come to the altar and get right with God?" With that he picked me up in his arms and started for the mourner's bench and carried me there and set me on it and prayed through that Sunday afternoon and he is now shouting in heaven, for he lived for God and never backslid. That was my first convert and, thank God, I have been trying to win men ever since. Is your ditch of love for souls cleaned out this afternoon? Have you dug one, or are you satisfied to go on and just live for yourself? Are you concerned about lost humanity? Have you lost your burden for souls, or is the burden as great as it ever was? Personally, I am living for nothing else these days but to win men and women for God. Everything else is lost in insignificance as far as I am concerned.

Some years ago I was going to a meeting in Philadelphia with the Nazarene people. As I was on my way to the meeting I was taken violently ill. They rushed me back to my home and put me to bed. I was in bed for two months and could not fill my engagements. At the end of two months, one Sunday afternoon my wife thought I was dying, and she called for the same doctor that I mentioned before. He said, "You will have to go to the hospital, but that will only give you temporary relief. Unless God heals you, you'll never preach like you have been preaching."

When he said that, my wife was sitting at the foot of the bed. My oldest sister, whom I had won to Christ, was sitting on the other side of the bed. She tiptoed her way out of the room. Three days later the saints were anointing me and praying for my healing. My sister was at home on her knees, and she was saying, "Oh, God, I can't preach; I don't have any talent to preach. I can't testify in meetings without breaking down and weeping. When they call on me to pray, I always break down and weep. There's my brother. Thou hast given him some ability to win souls, but the doctor says unless thou dost heal him, he will never preach again like he has been preaching." She continued, "Lord, I love souls. I want to be a soul-winner, but I don't have talent for it, and my brother does. If Thou will take that disease from my brother's body and put it in my body, I'm willing to die in his place that he might go on preaching the gospel."

God heard that prayer and touched my body, and I have never had a touch of that disease from that day until now. Six months later my sister came down with the same disease. They rushed her to a hospital in Philadelphia, put her on the operating table and gave her ether. She died while the doctor was operating. When I looked at her dead face in the casket and knew that she had taken my place and died that I might go on preaching and winning souls for God, I stood by that casket and looked up in the face of Jesus in the midst of that crowd and said, "Oh, God, if Thou wilt help me, I'll never live another day, nor preach another sermon but for the salvation of lost humanity."

God help us! I do not know why you are living, but I want to have souls to lay at the feet of Jesus Christ. If your ditches are not dug, why not dig them now so that God can have a channel to bless other lives through you? Will you do it now?

9

So Great Salvation

How shall we escape, if we neglect so great salvation? (Hebrews 2:3).
Behold, now is the accepted time; behold, now is the day of salvation (II Corinthians 6:2).

WE ARE SPEAKING ABOUT God's great salvation. The term *salvation* implies that there is something to be saved from as well as something to be saved to. In the spiritual realm it means to be saved from sin and hell and saved to God and heaven. The great salvation God has provided in Christ is perfect in its nature. Its nature makes it adaptable to our state and commensurate with our problem. It is adaptable to man's state only. It is not for angels or animals. It is planned to redeem man alone, and if other creatures or things are affected by it, they are affected only as a by-product and not a direct benefit. Man alone is the recipient of the atonement. It is commensurate with man's problem. Man's greatest problem is sin and salvation has met and dealt with that problem. Man has social, financial, and domestic problems, but Jesus Christ and his salvation are sufficient for every one of them.

Salvation is present in its application. It is revealed now. We do not know all that is embodied in the atonement, but we do have enough revealed for our salvation. It is offered now and must be received now. It is not to be received after death or in another world, but now. Now is the accepted time, and today is the day of salvation. It is this world that needs Christians, and not the world to come.

It is universal in its extent: "And he is the propitiation for our sins: and not for ours only, but also for the sins of the whole world" (I John 2:2). "For God so loved the world, that he gave his only begotten Son, that whosoever believeth in him should not perish, but have everlasting life" (John 3:16). "Ho, every one that thirsteth, come ye to the waters, and he that hath no money; come ye, buy, and eat" (Isaiah 55:1). Anything less than a "whosoever" salvation would be unworthy of God. Thank God! His gospel and his salvation are non-political and international.

It was on the island of Trinidad in the Port-of-Spain Pilgrim Holiness Church during a quarterly meeting. The people had gathered from many sections of that West Indian island to worship God. At the close of the service, scores were seeking him. We looked over that group of seekers and saw Chinese, Japanese, Portuguese, Guianese, West Indians, East Indians and Venezuelans. They were all seeking the same God. God met the need of each one in the salvation brought by Jesus Christ.

Salvation is free in its communication. It cannot be bought. It is something given, not something earned. It is never given on the basis of any qualification you may possess. It is by grace, and grace is the unmerited gift of God. It is granted through mercy, and mercy can only be extended to a guilty person. Real guilt can only be based on justice; therefore, salvation is based on justice, mercy and grace. Justice says we are guilty, but mercy sets aside justice and through the free gift of divine grace sets the sinner at liberty. The real dividing line between Calvinism and Arminianism may be here. It costs nothing except an acknowledgment of guilt, and if one will take this attitude toward Christ's salvation, there will not be enough devils in the universe to keep him from attaining it.

Christ's salvation is perfect in its nature, and it has a right to claim our examination. Its facts can stand our scrutiny. Everything else is changing, but not salvation, since it is founded upon eternal principles and facts.

Governments change from absolute monarchy to limited monarchy, from military autocracy to parliamentary democracy. Scientific knowledge expands until textbooks written today are out of date in just a few months, or at the longest, a few years. Educational methods change until instructors must be perpetual students to keep abreast of the times. But salvation ever abides the same in its processes and privileges.

It demands that you examine its necessity. It declares man is lost and can be found, or can find his way only in Jesus Christ. The reason for such a salvation is that man hopelessly disqualified himself as a child of God by disobedience, and he became a rebel against God's law. God could not by prerogative forgive him and take him back into fellowship. The law of God had been broken and justice demanded reparation. If justice demands, his love provides, and the facts of this will stand investigation by the most critical. Its provision, its power and its accomplishments are open for man's investigation. They have stood the tests of the ages and have been the anvil upon which many a hammer of unbelief has been worn out.

Salvation has a claim upon our consideration. God said, "O that they were wise, that they understood this, that they would consider their latter end!" (Deuteronomy 32:29) "Now therefore thus saith the Lord of hosts; consider your ways" (Haggai 1:5). Its facts should make anyone stop and consider. To ignore them and declare they are a myth does not do away with them. If they are a fact, then reason, natural instincts and the law of self-preservation all demand that we consider his salvation.

Salvation has a claim upon our diligence. Man has a soul to save, a heaven to gain, and a hell to shun. If God's Book is true and if his salvation is our only hope, then we should be careful not to neglect it. In the hills of Pennsylvania a rancher had purchased coal for a missionary church. When he went to pay for the coal, he found the man selling hard liquor. As he paid the bill, he said to the dealer, "Your soul is worth too much to be lost." That was all he said, but it stuck and soon the man was saved.

The little girl had it right when she climbed upon her father's knee after an insurance agent had been there and said, "Father, I heard you insure the house, the furniture and the car, but did you insure your soul?" Reader, is your soul saved? Has it been insured by the blood of Jesus Christ, or is it not worth your consideration?

How shall we escape degeneration? There is a universal principle that everything follows reversion to type. That is so in all of nature. We know that it is true with humanity. If a man neglects himself, he becomes a worse man. If he neglects his body, he becomes like an animal; if he neglects his mind, he becomes an illiterate; if he neglects his conscience, he becomes a moral renegade; if he neglects his soul, it atrophies and dies.

There are three great realms in which man lives: evolution, balance and decay.

A great preacher of the United States, Andrew Johnson, said, "Evolution is all right if you do not monkey with it." Evolution means, in reality, change for the better. It means hard work and constant industry. It means to keep at it and always at it to make improvement. Balance is to live along the line between evolution and decay—a precarious place. One step in the wrong direction may be disastrous. It is tightrope walking and cannot long be maintained by many people.

Decay is easy. In every man's nature the law of decay rules supreme. Give it full sway and you are lost. It is not natural to live; it is natural to die. It is natural to be bad; it is not natural to be good. Just as plants generate life or quicken death by the way they assimilate or repulse their environment, so man advances his moral, mental and spiritual life by the way he assimilates or repulses his environment. If a plant can assimilate them, they will start decay in the plant. The same is true with the spiritual man. If he can assimilate the Word of God, it will give him life; if he cannot assimilate it, it will bring death, for it is a savor of life unto life or death unto death. If one can take in Christ, he will become his life; if not, he will be ground to pieces by him.

How can one escape damnation? When we refuse to heed the things we have heard, neglect the things which give life, and play with sin that despoils the soul of its capacity for salvation, there is no escape from damnation. When we neglect the use of those faculties that can touch God, they become useless and die. It is said that in the great caverns of the earth the fish have places for eyes, but have no eyes. We are told the reason for this is that they have no use for their eyes and, therefore, have no eyes. If one should take his arm and strap it to his body and leave it there for a long time, useless, he would find it would be impossible to wiggle his fingers when the bandages were taken off. He would have to learn again to use the fingers, the hand and the arm. The same is true of the faculties that God has placed within the soul of man for his salvation. If he fails to use them in contacting God, they will shrivel up and die. When he does this, while salvation remains the same, he makes it of no effect by neglect.

How shall we escape if we neglect so great salvation? Neglect is so dangerous because one does not realize its deadly effect until it has accomplished its purpose. It is not always so much what man does that damns him as what he fails to do. He may not go out into the gross sins of the world and go to the depths of degradation; all he needs to do is to neglect salvation, and there is no escape for him from damnation.

10

Prayer

PRAYER IS MORE THAN a religious exercise; it is the Christian life. It is not simply uttering words; it is having strong desire. It is not more earnestness; it is groanings which cannot be uttered. It is not wrestling with God; it is prostration before God. Wrestling with God indicates rebellion, and one may come out of such a conflict crippled for life. Prostration before him reveals humility and he that humbleth himself shall be exalted. It is not preeminently seeking things from God; it is rather seeking God himself.

The greatest power in the hands of any man is the power of intercessory prayer. Plans and programs may accomplish things for this life, but prayer will accomplish things for both time and eternity. Jesus said, "I say unto you, that if two of you shall agree on earth as touching any thing that they shall ask, it shall be done for them of my Father which is in heaven," and "Whatsoever ye shall bind on earth shall be bound in heaven: and whatsoever ye shall loose on earth shall be loosed in heaven." In this Jesus shows that intercessory prayer not only effects things in time, but also in eternity. It is a key which forever locks or unlocks. The greatest personalities in politics and industry can tie up things only for a time; but the saints, if they will pray, can bind things for eternity.

In Luke, the eleventh chapter, there is an account of the disciples asking Jesus to teach them to pray and the record of Jesus' compliance. In his teaching on that occasion, he suggested the place, the plan, the parable, the promise, the purpose, the possibilities and the problems of prayer.

The Place of Prayer

"But thou, when thou prayest, enter into thy closet, and when thou hast shut thy door, pray to thy Father which is in secret; and thy Father which seeth in secret shall reward thee openly." The closet may be any place where one can be alone with God. People may be all around, but one can shut himself away from even the one with whom he may be rubbing elbows. When one tries to get the door shut, he may find all kinds of pestering things trying to get past, but successful praying can never be done until the door is closed and all wandering thoughts, worldly ambitions and wrong desires are on the outside. It is only as one is shut in alone with God that God can reveal himself. It is in the secret place of the Most High that one abides under the shadow of the Almighty. Great characters are built in solitude, and spiritual strength is gathered when alone in God's presence. While this is true, it would be a waste of God-invested strength to remain forever in the closet alone with God. To test one's development there must be contacts with the enemy; but when the conflict comes, "Thy Father which seeth in secret shall reward thee openly."

> *Take time to be holy,*
> *Speak oft with thy Lord;*
> *Abide in him always,*
> *And feed on his Word.*

The Plan of Prayer

The Lord's Prayer, or as it is also called, the Kingdom Prayer, was not meant to be listlessly and indifferently repeated by sinners. It was given as a model for all prayer. No one can honestly repeat it except true children of God; and they do not just repeat it, they pray it. Notice its construction as given in Matthew 6:9-13. "Our Father." Who can address him thus but his children? Here is real relationship. "Hallowed be Thy Name." It is not a glib, light, repeating of something, but a real heartfelt reverence. Men who utter this prayer must, then, at the very first give up what to most people is the dearest thing on earth, their name; for one loses his own identity and becomes identified with Christ.

"Thy kingdom come." One's own little house crumbles and his ambitions lie in the dust. One must stop seeking to build anything whatsoever for himself and put Christ's cause first. It is here one is taught to seek first the kingdom of God. It is here all rights to one's self are released, and Jesus Christ takes over the throne of one's life, exercising his rights as Lord. "Thy will be done." This is more than complacent resignation which says, "Because it is the will of God, I shall submit to it;" but it is joyful and delightful renunciation of self such as expressed in the words, "Lo, I come . . . to do thy will, O God," and again when Jesus says, "My meat is to do the will of him that sent me." It is not an annihilation of one's will, but a cooperation of the human will with the divine. It is where but to know his will is to obey it. It is where the will of God is done cheerfully, quickly and without controversy.

"Give us this day our daily bread." Here is utter dependence upon him for temporal and physical needs as well as for the "bread of life." "Forgive us our trespasses (or debts) as we forgive those who trespass against us." What unworthiness! No one can pray this until he knows he is right with all men. "Lead us not into temptation." The reason many people fall is because they stay too close to temptation. It is so with Eve, with David, and with Judas. One should always pray to be led away from temptation. If God ever does maneuver things to place one near temptation, it is more to test than to tempt, and he will with the temptation "make a way of escape." "But deliver us from evil." This is a request for heart purity. A desire to be delivered from the source of evil, inbred sin. "For thine is the kingdom, and the power and the glory." The answer to one's prayer should be sought because it is God's work one is interested in, because God has the power and it will be for his glory.

A Parable of Prayer

A parable of prayer is found in Luke 11:5-8. What a picture it presents! There is a good man seeking a good thing for a good purpose. There is another good man with apparent indifference holding him off with a confusing excuse. This depicts the seeming indifference of God, at times, to the cry of his children. There is a man who is a friend, but he is in trouble in a dark hour. He has someone looking to him for help, but he has nothing within himself by which to satisfy the need. For help he goes to the best and only source he knows and finds what looks like beclouded friendship and indifference. How confused and helpless he must have felt at his friend's reply; but he knows there is no other help, so he hangs on.

Doubtless most believers in a dark and needy hour have come to God, only to find what seemed like indifference. How confused and helpless it makes one feel! In fact, God has perhaps seemed to completely ignore the prayer, and his silence was almost more than one could bear. The temptation has come to question his purpose, love and friendship. But how happy has been the result if one did not yield to that temptation but kept pressing his way right into God's presence, yes, right unto God himself until the answer has come.

Many times God's silence is hard to understand, but it is usually prolonged until God can find a place where he can give a greater revelation of himself. This is so evident in Jesus' silence when he knew that Lazarus was sick, and again when he knew he was dead. He did not rush to comfort the sorrowing, but tarried with his disciples. He even told his disciples that he was glad for their sakes that he was not there to the intent they might believe. Although his slowness to go to his sorrowing friends may have been confusing to his disciples, his purpose was that they might receive a lesson of faith. One should learn from this parable never to let go of God no matter how dark the night or how urgent the need or how silent the heavens, for he declares this man won out by persistence, finally receiving all that he needed.

The Promise of Prayer

Immediately after this parable of prayer with all of its implications, Jesus gives the promise of prayer. "Ask, and it shall be given you; seek, and ye shall find; knock, and it shall be opened unto you; For everyone that asketh, receiveth; and he that seeketh, findeth; and to him that knocketh it shall be opened." In the three verses which follow there seems to be ground for the fulfillment of these verses. That ground is one's relationship to God, his righteousness and his resources.

If one is a recognized child of God, he can expect not only an answer but exactly what is needed and asked. If a son shall ask bread of any that is a father, will he give him a stone for bread, a serpent for fish, or a scorpion for an egg? Not if he is a true father. When once one recognizes he is a child of God and that God is his Father, it prohibits all questioning about what he will do in his case.

In Second Corinthians, the sixth chapter, there are five things mentioned which one must give up before God will recognize him. Then there are five things he will become to him or do for him. One must come out from among the world, touch not the unclean things, be not unequally yoked together with unbelievers, have no part with an infidel and have no agreement with idols. When people comply with this, they have the promise from God, "I will receive you, and will be a father unto you, and ye shall be my sons and daughters." How say some, then, that they cannot receive the Holy Ghost? There is only one real reason that can keep one from receiving the Holy Spirit and that is the lack of sonship. "If ye then, being evil, know how to give good gifts unto your children: how much more shall your heavenly Father give the Holy Spirit to them that ask him?"

The righteousness of God demands an answer to prayer. God seems to imply, "If you are evil and yet you will not withhold any good gift from your child, then how could I be righteous and withhold any good gift from my children? My righteousness will make me do it, if nothing else."

The resources of God make the answer sure. Again it is as if he were saying, "If you in your little sphere will go your limit to give good gifts to your children, then for me to be a Father, I must go to my limit to give good gifts to my children; and if I go the limit of my resources, then there is nothing you can ask but what I can supply." The apostles gave glory "unto him that is able to do exceeding abundantly above all that we ask or think, according to the power that worketh in us," indicating that the only limit is one's capacity. Again, Paul assured his fellow Christians, "My God shall supply all your need according to his riches in glory by Christ Jesus." No one has ever been able to take inventory of that stock of resources.

The Purpose of Prayer

There are many by-products of prayer, but only one major purpose. One minor purpose or by-product is to use prayer as a source of supply for personal needs. If it be true that "your father knoweth what things ye have need of, before ye ask him," why ask? Certainly not primarily to have needs supplied, if he already knows what is needed. There must be a deeper reason.

Another minor purpose is for the success of one's work. It is all right to pray about this, and one must pray about it; but, after all, Paul plants and Apollos waters, but God gives the increase. The Scripture here is indicating that if one does his part that God will surely do his.

One does not have to beg God to do it, for he has obligated himself to do it when man's part is finished.

Another minor purpose, though of more importance than those already mentioned, is to positionize man in his relation to God and things. The motto, "Prayer changes things," is not always literally true. The truth is, prayer changes man in his relationship to God and in his attitude to things. When Moses came down from the Mount and found Israel singing and dancing around the golden calf, with God's anger stirred against them he immediately broke the tables of stone on which God had written the Ten Commandments. Thus Israel was taken out from under the penalty of the law of God which, if executed, would have meant their total destruction.

Then Moses stepped in the breach to save them. When God told him to get out of the way and he would blot Israel off the face of the earth and make of Moses a great nation, Moses said, "Yet now, if thou wilt forgive their sin . . .; and if not, blot me, I pray thee, out of thy book which thou hast written." Immediately there was a change in the relation of Israel to God. God must deal with them on different grounds than simply that of a broken law. A new element had entered into the case which God must reckon with—that is, substitution and intercessory prayer. Intercessory prayer founded in redemption by substitution will certainly change men in their relation to God and God in his attitude toward men.

Prayer changes man in his attitude to things. Many times one prays for God to change conditions which seem unbearable, but they remain the same year after year. Sometimes he enables one to change them. A case in point is the incident when Israel stood before Ai. Joshua prayed for victory, and God told him to get up and clean house and victory would come. God would not change the condition, but he did enable Joshua to do it. There are times, however, when God does not change conditions, neither does he enable his believers to change them, but he does change one's attitude toward them so that they are not so hard to bear. The change is not in the condition, but in the one who is praying. The change in the one who prays may be so great that he can not only bear the unbearable with good grace, but he can come to say with Paul, "We glory in tribulation also," and "I take pleasure in infirmities, in re-

proaches, in necessities, in persecutions, in distresses for Christ's sake."
How unnatural, but how glorious!

The major purpose of prayer, however, is to feed one's soul on the life
of God. Salvation is not an experience only; it is a life. That life must be
fed. The best channel through which it can be fed is prayer. It is while in
prayer that the human spirit feeds on God himself. There is nothing in
the universe but God that will feed man's spirit. The spirit of man can
live only by the Spirit of God. As the spirit takes its life from God, it
develops into a channel through which God can accomplish things. One
rejoices to see things coming to pass which he has desired. But how
much greater would be the joy, if he could but see the change that has
been wrought within himself which makes it possible for God to do such
things through him!

One should not pray simply to change or obtain things or to attain
success. He should pray so as to enter farther into God until in God he
does very literally live and move and have his being. One should so pray
that God can help himself to one's life as he sees fit. Then it is that things
will be given, changes will come, and success will attend one's activities
as the by-product of a God-fed life.

The Possibilities of Prayer

Here is a realm never yet fully explored. If men would so feed upon
God that he could enlarge them to the extent that he could have channels
big enough to give him even elbow room, there would be no limits to the
possibilities of prayers. Its possibilities are limited only by men's dwarfed
spiritual lives. One cannot force the great Niagara through a one-inch
pipe and expect it to run great power plants. No more can one force God
through a shriveled-up soul and expect repetitions of Pentecost, even in
miniature. When Abraham prayed for Sodom, God went as far with him
as the life of God in Abraham would permit. Had the life of God in him
been fed enough so that his faith channel was large enough, Sodom might
have been spared. His weakness caused failure just one step short of
victory. When Moses prayed for Israel, he had been feeding on God for
forty days. There was no trace of weakness, so there was no limit to what
God could and would do. When Joshua prayed for the sun to stand still,
God found in him a channel large enough to transmit sufficient power to

stop it in its course. When Elijah prayed for rain, he prayed seven times before the life of God in him was strong enough for God to use it as a lever to unbolt the windows of heaven.

There is only one limit to the possibility of prayer, and that is the weakness of the life of God in man. Paul said, "I can do all things through Christ which strengtheneth me." In other words, if one has fed on Christ until he is strong enough, he can do all things. "All things are possible to him that believeth."

The Problems of Prayer

There are different kinds of prayer. There is the prayer of the impenitent sinner which consists of so many words and phrases, but afterwards it leaves the one praying just where it found him. Then there is the prayer of the penitent, such as that offered by the publican, "Lord, be merciful to me a sinner." There is the prayer of the backslider such as that in the fifty-first Psalm, "I acknowledge my transgression: and my sin is ever before me." Such prayers usually get results, for they are usually accompanied with a broken and a contrite spirit which the Lord will not despise. There is also the prayer of the believer for heart purity, as found in Psalm 51:10, "Create in me a clean heart, O God." There is a prayer of the child of God for the supply of physical and material needs. And, finally, there is the prayer of the intercessor who goes to the garden alone with Christ and fellowships his sufferings as he agonizes for a lost world. How few there are who ever reach this realm! So few, in fact, that the Bible declares that God was astonished that there was no intercessor. The spiritual realm in which one finds himself may be because of the problem in his prayer life.

One problem may be that he does not measure up to the laws of prayer. Wherever God's laws are found—whether regarding the rocks, the flowers, the stars, the tides, or spiritual matters—they function perfectly. If those laws are perfectly obeyed, they will produce perfect results. There are certain laws covering one's prayer life which, if not obeyed, will hinder one in getting answers to prayer.

The first to be considered here is the law of sincerity. "If I regard iniquity in my heart, the Lord will not hear me." Covered sin in any degree will certainly hinder prayer.

Wrong attitudes toward one's wife, husband, children, parents, or other relatives, or neighbors, preachers or laymen will cause the heavens to be shut. Even an over indulgence in legitimate things such as eating, sleeping, taking recreation, and visiting may keep one from getting his prayers answered.

Another law is that of abiding. Jesus said, "If ye abide in me, and my words abide in you, ye shall ask what ye will, and it shall be done unto you." Fluctuations in one's Christian profession will close God's ear to one's cry. God loves consistency and constancy. He wants his children in their Christian lives to be like the boy who, when asked what his name was, answered, "It is Billy." When asked if it was Billy Sunday, he replied, "No, it is Billy everyday." God wants us to be Christians every day, not just on Sunday. "And my words abide in you" indicated that not only is one to live according to the Book every day, but he is to present his petitions through the promises of the Book. What he has not promised, there is no use to ask. If he had not confined his answers to his promises, there would be danger of man running wild in his petitioning. If one stays within God's promises in asking, then he will not suffer so much from the depression of unanswered prayer.

Another law is that of relationship. "If ye then, being evil, know how to give good gifts unto your children: how much more shall your heavenly Father give the Holy Spirit to them that ask him?" There are some prayers that can be answered only on the grounds of relationship. One of them is the prayer for the fullness of the Holy Spirit. There is no need for even a penitent sinner to ask for this. It is an inheritance and an inheritance is given on the ground of family relationship only. An outsider may give a legacy, but it takes a relative to leave an inheritance. Therefore, for a sinner to pray for this would be a waste of time. If one is in the family, however, it ought not be so much trouble for him to get his inheritance. One needs to but prove his relationship and it is his.

Another law is the law of agreement. "I say unto you, That if two of you shall agree on earth as touching anything that they shall ask, it shall be done for them of my Father which is in heaven." This agreement must be in desire as well as in asking; and it must be for God's glory, for James says, "Ye ask, and receive not, because ye ask amiss, that ye may consume it upon your lusts." Wrong motives and wrong desires in asking will hinder the answer to prayer.

Then there is the law of faith. "Whatsoever ye shall ask in prayer, believing, ye shall receive." On earth when Jesus was here and people petitioned him, he always pried into their faith life. His reply was, in substance, "How is your faith? If your faith is all right, you may have it." "According to your faith be it unto you."

Then there is the law of obedience. This is implied in all of God's promises. No promise in this age is unconditional. If man will do certain things, then God says he will do certain things. There is no need to pray until one has done his part; and remember that God never does what he commands man to do. All of one's sacrifices, all of one's faithfulness in attending church, all of one's visiting of the sick, all of the display of talent will never take the place of obedience. "Behold, to obey is better than sacrifice, and to hearken than the fat of rams."

There may be some other hindrances to prayer over which one does not have direct control. Men can hinder the fulfillment of prayer or one's friends may pray contrary to the desired request, or Satan may hinder, as in the case of Daniel. But all of these will be finally overcome if one will live up to the laws which govern prayer.

11

Hindered Prayers

MAN IS AN EXTREMIST when it comes to seeking after power. We hear talk of the power of education, the power of organization, the power of money, the power of machinery, the power of tools, the power of politics, the power in alliances and the power in atoms. But comparatively little is heard of the power in prayer. Nevertheless, there is power in prayer to shut the mouths of lions and quench the burning of fire; to dry up the flow of rivers; make the sun stand still in its orbit; to change the course of nations and empires; to heal the sick and raise the dead; to shut up the heavens when rain was needed; to move God to wrath against his enemies and to stay his hand when it has been raised in anger.

The things prayer has wrought, if all were written, would fill more books than one could read in a lifetime; but the things that it might have wrought and has not because it has not been used, or is not being used, would fill many more books. Why men do not use this Power and why they knowingly permit things to interfere with its effects is a mystery hard to clarify. Whatever else we may say about it, we must admit it is a source of mighty power going to waste which, if properly used, might revolutionize earth and heaven.

Notice some things which hinder answers to prayer. Selfishness. "Ye ask, and receive not, because ye ask amiss, that ye may consume it upon your lusts" (James 4:3). There are many ways in which men seek to gratify their desires and pleasures, but when men use prayer for that purpose, it becomes disgusting. Prayer is certainly a shallow affair when thus used simply to seek a selfish blessing. But there is too much selfish praying. If all is going well, too often men have little time to pray. When adversity comes, they flee to the refuge of the secret closet of prayer. That is selfish praying. When one waits for sickness, death or losses of any kind to drive him to his knees, that is selfish praying. When one's prayers begin and end with his needs, his family, his church, his denomination or the particular work in which he is engaged, that praying is selfish and such prayers are hindered by the spirit of the one offering the prayer.

Fallen Angels

This is one source of difficulty in prayer that man is in no way responsible for and yet it may be the cause of many unanswered prayers. In the tenth chapter of the book of Daniel we have a picture of an answer to prayer being hindered for twenty-one days. Daniel was troubled over a vision. He sought God for an answer. On the twenty-first day one like unto the Son of Man in appearance stood before him and said, "Fear not, Daniel; for from the first day that thou didst set thine heart to understand, and to chasten thyself before thy God, thy words were heard, and I am come for thy words. But the prince of the kingdom of Persia withstood me one and twenty days: but, lo, Michael, one of the chief princes, came to help me; and I remained there with the kings of Persia." Here we see that this one who was like unto the Son of Man informed Daniel that the first day he began to pray his prayers were heard and the answer was started on the way, but that he, the messenger, was hindered by the prince of Persia and only got through with the message because Michael, the chief angel over the Jews, came to his help.

Here is a great truth and, perhaps, a great mystery. It seems that Satan is in charge of all Gentile nations and that he has placed one of his princes over each nation. Here we have one placed over Persia and another over Grecia. It seems that the only nation that had a good angel to guard it was the Jewish nation and that angel was called Michael. It seems there are battles in the aerial regions that humanity knows nothing about; battles between God's angels and those of the devil; battles over souls, battles to change the course of nations, battles to destroy God's people, and battles to keep prayers from being answered. When prayer is unanswered, it is well to search for the cause. If the cause cannot be found in one's self, then one may be quiet in the rest of faith, knowing that God is trying to fight his way through with the answer.

Ignorance in Asking

We are told in the Book of God that in our praying we know not what we should ask for as we should, but the Spirit helpeth our infirmities. Prayer out of the Spirit may be so ignorant of real desire and real needs that God must maintain his intelligence and ignore it. When one listens to some public praying, he is made to wonder how an intelligent God is going to answer such prayers and not be counted foolish in the sight of men. So foolish are some public prayers that one is made to wonder if those prayers are not directed more to the audience than to God. To pray intelligently one must have imagination, strong desire, fervency of spirit and be aided by the Holy Ghost; and if the Holy Ghost does not lend aid to one's prayers, they will not be answered.

Lack of Importunity

Joseph Smith used to say that the verse, "Pray without ceasing" (I Thessalonians 5:17), means when one starts to pray for things, he should never stop until he gets it. That, perhaps, is a good interpretation. Importunity is one of the most important factors in successful praying. There are two great illustrations of this in Scripture. The one is found in Luke 18:1-8. There Jesus gives a parable known to Bible readers as the Parable of the Unjust Judge. It draws a picture of a widow going to the judge and saying,

> "Avenge me of mine adversary." And he would not for a while: but afterward he said within himself, "Though I fear not God, nor regard man; yet because this widow troubleth me, I will avenge her, lest by her continual coming she weary me." And the Lord said, "Hear what the unjust judge saith. And shall not God avenge his own elect, which cry day and night unto him, though he bear long with them?"

We know that in this parable Jesus is teaching the lesson of importunity. For the first verse of this chapter says, "And he spake a parable unto them to this end, that men ought always [not just once in a while, but always] to pray, and not to faint."

The other picture is found in Luke 11 where a man having a friend as a visitor calls at his home in the night. In going to his cupboard to find something to give his visiting friend and finding nothing, he went to his neighbor and called him from his bed, begging for bread with which to feed the visitor.

He said, "For a friend of mine in his journey is come to me, and I have nothing to set before him." And then his request, "Friend, lend me three loaves."

Here we have one of the best pictures of successful praying in the Bible. Here we have honesty, for he said, "I have nothing to set before him." We have unselfishness; he is asking his friend to lend him three loaves, not for himself, not for his own family, but for another. He did not ask for a handout; he expected to make a return. He did not want something for nothing. Then we have humility: "I have nothing to set before him." What a confession that was on the part of the solicitor. Then we have definiteness. He said, "Lend me three loaves." He knew how many he needed and did not ask for more or less. As his friend hesitated to arise from his bed and give him, he did not change the request; it was always for three loaves. How often we change our prayers! If we do not get them through the first time, we will change our expression and our request. We lower them because our faith is lowering as the answer is delayed.

The two portrayals give a vivid idea of what is meant by the last step—importunity. The friend from whom he sought three loaves said, "Trouble me not; the door is now shut, and my children are with me in bed; I cannot rise and give thee," but he would not leave until he had received what he was after. What would be wrought through prayer if we had more praying after this pattern!

Lack of Consistent Living

In I Peter 3:7 we read, "Likewise, ye husbands, dwell with them according to knowledge, giving honor unto the wife, as unto the weaker vessel, and as being heirs together of the grace of life; that your prayers be not hindered." Here we are informed that living contrary to known duty will hinder prayer from being answered.

Often we have heard men praying in public whose lives we knew were crooked. But those men have climbed to such heights in phraseology that the people were brought to a stage of excitement that was uncontrollable and called it the blessing of God. Was that an answer to prayer or a result of psychology? If a man does not live righteous, can he be really blessed of God? One wonders if we have not placed more of a premium on good feelings than on straight living. Too often a sermon that makes us feel good is considered to be a great sermon, whether it inspires us to live right or not. A prayer that stirs our emotions is too often considered a great prayer, whether it ever gets an answer or not. The blessing of God always attends a stand for righteousness. Emotionalism may not be necessary to successful praying. An impenitent man who continues to live in sin may receive an answer to prayer, but not to his prayer. He may receive what he asked for, but it was not his praying that brought it.

Lack of Faith

Jesus said, "According to your faith, so be it unto you." One cannot receive anything from God without exercising faith. Without faith it is impossible to please him, and certainly one could not expect him to answer his prayers while he is displeasing him. "All things are possible to him that believeth." Faith is taking God at his Word and acting like he meant it. If our prayers were not so wordy but a little more meaty with faith, more would be accomplished. The greatest men this world have ever known were men of childlike faith. That statement of Jesus means more to me each day of my life:

> At the same time came the disciples unto Jesus, saying, "Who is the greatest in the kingdom of heaven?" And Jesus called a little child unto him, and set him in the midst of them, and said, "Verily I say unto you, except ye be converted, and become as little children, ye shall not enter into the kingdom of heaven."

To be childlike in love, in hate, in malice, in trust and in faith.

> *If our faith were but more simple*
> *We would take him at his Word.*

Faith and obedience will bring an answer to our prayers every time. I did not say the answer would always be a "yes," but faith and obedience will bring an answer.

12

A Good Conscience

MUCH HAS BEEN WRITTEN about the conscience, and authors have differed so widely regarding its nature that most men are left in doubt as to what the conscience really is. Some authorities speak of it as "God in man;" others refer to it as "God's Umpire" or "a judge" and still others call it "the eye of the soul." Numerous other different definitions have also been presented which make the matter somewhat confusing for many people. While it may not be possible to define it to everyone's satisfaction, it is no doubt possible to get some light on its purpose, its power and its progress.

Its Purpose

Perhaps a good way to discover the purpose of the human conscience is to approach the matter negatively and to first find out what its purpose is not. Its purpose is certainly not to point out the way of salvation. Every normal human being, whether born in a Christian or a heathen land, has a conscience. If conscience could lead men to salvation, there would be no need for the Bible, the Holy Spirit or human agents. As far as is known, there has never been a real work of salvation without either the Bible, the Holy Spirit or a human teacher. Usually it takes all three. Conscience alone cannot lead men into salvation.

Its purpose is not even to point out to men the path of moral right. Men have been known to do the most vile deeds without their conscience functioning in any way relative to the unrighteousness. Men in religious work have been known to engage in the most degrading immoral practices without any stirring of conscience. Jesus said that a man might even kill another and, in so doing, think he was doing God's service. This is not necessarily because men have seared their conscience, but because the natural conscience is not meant to be a guide in moral matters any more than it is in spiritual matters.

According to Scripture it would seem that the purpose of conscience is to witness.

> For when the Gentiles, which have not the law, do by nature the things obtained in the law, these, having not the law, are a law unto themselves: which shew the work of the law written in their hearts, their conscience also bearing witness, and their thoughts the mean while accusing or else excusing one another (Romans 2:14, 15).

Reference is here made to people in the dim light of a natural law written in their hearts. It is certainly reasonable to conclude that not all of the law of God was written in their heart; for had it been, there would have been no need for God to have written it on tables of stone. The law of God written in the natural heart is very dim in comparison with the law of God written in his Word. The unenlightened man can only know what is right and wrong in his relation to another in his family, tribal or national life, as his native law points it out and conscience either accuses or excuses the man who breaks that law.

"And they which heard it, being convicted by their own conscience, went out one by one, beginning at the eldest, even unto the last" (John 8:9). Here is a picture of a group of Jews demanding the execution of the penalty for breaking their law against adultery. Jesus told them if they had not broken any of their laws to go ahead with the execution. Their consciences at once functioned, witnessing against them, and they walked off. Conscience did not tell them what was right or wrong. Their law had done that, but conscience witnessed against them when they broke the law.

"I say the truth in Christ, I lie not, my conscience also bearing me witness in the Holy Ghost" (Romans 9:1). Here is a Christian under the blazing light of the Gospel of Jesus Christ, as revealed by the indwelling presence of the Holy Ghost, declaring that his conscience witnessed that what he had done was right.

Conscience is not a guide to the natural man to show him right from wrong. The natural law, written in his heart, does that, and unless he murders his conscience, it will function as a witness every time he crosses that law. It will either excuse him or accuse him. The sad part is that, as far as is known, the light of that natural law has been so dim that it has never been sufficient to lead men to Christ.

Conscience was not the guide to the Jew to show him right from wrong. His law did that, and conscience stepped in only as a witness against him when he broke that law and to witness in his favor when he kept the law. Conscience is not the guide to the Christian. The work of God in the Bible as it is revealed by the Holy Ghost tells him what is right and what is wrong. It approves when it is kept and it condemns when it is broken.

It is often said, "Conscience is not a safe guide." Conscience is not a guide at all. It is a witness, and a witness only functions after an act has been committed or the decision to commit that act has been finally made.

Its Power

If conscience were a judge—as some have called it—with the power to sentence just as it has the power as a witness to condemn, it might at once plunge its victims into hell. But God has never delegated to it that power. If it had the power to convert as it has the power to convict, it would control and convert the world. But it does not have that power.

Its power is, however, so great that it has scaled the highest habitable mountains, crossed the largest continents, spanned every trackless mountain, crossed the largest continents, spanned every trackless ocean, girdled the globe and annihilated space to run down its victims. Time has never been able to successfully hush its voice and eternity will only quicken its torments. Its accusing voice has no doubt done as much to bring about adjustments of wrongs as any other power on earth. It made a king quake with fear, as an unknown hand wrote dark sentences on his palace wall; it caused a judge to tremble before his shackled prisoner; it forced a ruler to declare that the preacher he had murdered to please the ungodly had returned to life; and it prompted the woman at the well, to whom Christ had pointed out only one sin, to say that he had told her all things that she had ever done. No person who ever crosses the light coming from the law under which he is living can escape its accusing finger and voice.

Its Progress

Conscience may progress downward or it may make upward progress. Notice, first, its downward progress. The first step in its downward progress is a wound. "But when ye sin so against the brethren, and wound their weak conscience, ye sin against Christ" (I Corinthians 8:12). Here is a conscience being wounded and unable to function properly because the light of God's truth was dimmed in the hearts of some by the careless thoughtless actions of others. Those who knew it was wrong to eat meat offered unto idols, had they been left to themselves, their consciences would have properly functioned as a witness against them when they partook of such meat. While watching others eat in the idol temple, they concluded they were eating meat offered to idols and decided if others could, they could do likewise.

In making such a decision, they wounded their consciences by walking in the light of the actions of others rather than in the light of God's command. This brings about a weakness of conscience which is serious and lowers the bars to let many things come into one's life that hitherto were forbidden. It is dangerous to take one's eyes from the Word of God as revealed by the Holy Ghost and place them on the actions of men as one's standard of guidance. It will always wound and weaken one's conscience.

The next step downward is a defiled conscience. "And their conscience being weak is defiled" (I Corinthians 8:7). Slimed over with guilt but with no power within himself to take away the filth, he therefore goes step by step on the downward path adding slime to slime and filth to filth.

The next step downward is an evil conscience. "Let us draw near with a true heart in full assurance of faith, having our hearts sprinkled from an evil conscience" (Hebrews 10:22). Just how such a conscience functions, Scripture does not reveal and certainly it is not safe to trust as a witness; it would always be telling one that he was right, even though he were wrong, according to the light of the law under which he lived. Were this not the case, it could not be termed an evil conscience.

The next step downward is a seared conscience. "Speaking lies in hypocrisy; having their consciences seared with a hot iron" (I Timothy 4:2). These people had departed from it so far, by trampling on the condemning voice of conscience, that they could not only do things contrary to the Word of God without feeling the pangs of an accusing conscience, but they could teach others to do likewise. They could even practice doctrines of devils and feel they were doing God's service.

One should not depend on conscience and feel safe simply because it does not condemn him, unless he is in the Holy Ghost and walking in all the light he has given him through his Word.

It is not necessary to be always going downward; it is possible to make upward progress in the development of a good conscience. Unless one has seared his conscience until it has utterly abandoned its functions, there is a way to start in that upward direction.

The first step is found in Hebrews 9:14: "How much shall the blood of Christ, who through the eternal spirit offered himself without spot to God, purge your conscience from dead works to serve the living God." This purging takes place in regeneration. It is not cleansing from carnality, but from the apathy and deadness which grips the conscience of the person who depends upon works to save him. Such a person may disobey the revealed Word of God and thus bring his conscience to witness against him, but ever against that he places his good works which are called by Paul "dead" because they have no saving virtue. That man hushes his conscience while he justifies his wrong act with the argument that he is doing some good works. Paul says God can take the load of dead works from such a conscience by a process of purging through the blood of Christ, so that the conscience can function properly and not be encumbered by the dead works but will be out in the clear while serving the living God.

The next upward step would naturally be a pure conscience and this is spoken of in connection with faith. Paul writes of it in I Timothy 3:9: "Holding the mystery of the faith in a pure conscience." This is primarily spoken of in reference to the teaching of sound doctrine. Under the influence of a seared conscience men will teach almost any damnable heresy, but with a pure conscience men will teach nothing but the truth of God as revealed to them by the Holy Ghost, especially in reference to personal experience. Paul had a great deal of trouble with teachers who contended for the law and kept the people in confusion relative to their standing with God, but he said teachers who had a pure conscience under the light of the Gospel would hold to the mystery of faith. Not only will that light make one hold to the mystery of faith in doctrine, but in practice as well. God, give us more people living by the law of faith which worketh by love! Too many now live by the letter of the law kept in a show of will worship which in the end bringeth legality, formality, lifelessness, coldness and death.

The third step upward is a good conscience. Acts 23:1 reads, "And Paul, earnestly beholding the council, said, 'Men and brethren, I have lived in all good conscience before God until this day.'" Some have said that Paul lied when he said that, but he certainly did not. What he said he had done has been repeated in the lives of countless hundreds. Many have gone contrary to the will of God and have had not guilt on the conscience. A good conscience is not always a safe conscience.

Paul had done many things contrary to the teachings of Christ, had even gone so far as to try to kill the Christians, and yet his conscience did not witness against him. Why? He was living under the light of the law while he was persecuting the Christians, and he says that as touching the law he was blameless. When light shined on him while on the road to Damascus and he received a divine revelation of God's will under the new dispensation, he stopped at once and faced the blazing light of the Gospel. While living under the law, he had walked in all good conscience before God until that day, because he had lived up to every ray of light he had had. Although he had done some things contrary to the will of God, he did not know it at the time. Men may, without a troubled conscience, do many things condemned by God in his Book because the truth of the Book has never been revealed to them by the Holy Ghost.

The fourth step forward is a conscience void of offense toward God and toward man. "And herein do I exercise myself, to have always a conscience void of offense toward God, and toward man" (Acts 24:16). This verse implies there is some exercising to be done to keep such a conscience. To walk in all the light God gives is not the work of an indolent person. As one walks in the light or refuses to walk in it, conscience works to keep up to either approve or to disapprove.

Someone has said there is such a thing as an "underworked conscience" and an "overworked conscience." That can hardly be possible. It is not underworked, for it works always with all the power it has. It is never overworked, for unless it has been wounded, weakened, made evil or seared, its strong constitution is able to witness against one every time he fails to live up to present light. Often people are called "over-conscientious." It is not conscience that is troubling them at all, but they are in heaviness because they have crossed some unscriptural teaching they have received or because they have crossed some personal notion not founded in the Word of God. As a child of God, one's conscience will only condemn him when he has crossed the Word of God as revealed by the Holy Ghost. All other heaviness of feelings which come are from some other source and do not break one's fellowship with God.

How may a conscience void of offense toward God and toward man be maintained? In order to keep a conscience void of offense, one must act in accordance to whatever God has revealed to him through his Word—whether it refers to things to do or things to leave undone. What God reveals through his Word may seem unreasonable, but conscience will approve. What God forbids may be pleasing in one's own sight and one cannot understand why a loving God should not want him to enjoy what seems to be harmless and beneficial. To refuse some things may bring a laugh from one's friends and scorn from one's enemies, but approval from one's conscience.

To cross the Word of God as revealed by the Holy Ghost is not a small matter, for it is sin. It takes only one sin to make one's conscience condemn him and, if an enlightened conscience condemns, God as the great Judge will sentence to damnation unless proper adjustments are made. To override the enlightened conscience, hush its voice for the present, and thus dim the light of revealed truth results in disaster at the judgment.

Remember that when the Holy Ghost reveals truth, he reveals it by truth. Under his light life must be adjusted. When he reveals truth, he reveals the right principles upon which all truth is founded, and any man living by the right principles underlying truth will never act because of expediency. It is a great weakness to fear what happens if one does right and, therefore, compromise principles for expediency.

If, because of pressure from friends, loved ones or church leaders, one has made a decision to do something which crosses the Word of God and conscience witnesses that the decision is wrong, do not argue with it. Reverse your decision at once. When in doubt about a moral action, do nothing until assured God's Word gives the green light to go ahead or the read light to stop; then act according to the signal, and by so doing keep a conscience void of offense toward God and toward man.

13

The Price of Fellowship

THE CHRISTIAN LIFE IS not indoctrination, but regeneration. It is not imitation; it is impartation. It is not reaching out after an idea; it is identifying oneself with Jesus Christ. It is not asking God to give something; it is letting God make something out of one. It is not asking God to give one power to carry out his own program; it is letting God use one in his divine program. It is not asking God to take a hand in one's personal interest; it is identifying oneself with his interest. It is not license to do as one pleases; it is letting God have liberty in one's life to do with one as he pleases. It is not walking in the light of one's neighbor; it is walking in the light as he, Christ, is in the light. "If we walk in the light, as he is in the light, we have fellowship one with another."

It is right at this point that there is much backsliding and broken fellowship. When one is saved, it is a change from darkness to light. "For ye were sometimes darkness; but now are ye light in the Lord, walk as children of light." To keep out of darkness, one must continue to keep step with his light. The price of fellowship with Jesus Christ or his people is to continuously bring the lowest point in one's living up to the top on one's light. One cannot live below present light and still fellowship with him.

The question, "What is light?" naturally presents itself. Someone has said that there are two kinds of spiritual light: one being specific and the other general. Specific light is light which an individual alone may have. If obeyed, it will prohibit him from doing some things others may do. It is as one walks in this light that he may, unless he is very careful, become critical of those who can do things which he cannot do. Such a person will need to be careful that it is real light and not just some notion he is following. It should be remembered that all spiritual light comes to one by some truth being applied to the heart by the Holy Ghost. If this has not been so, then what some people term *light* may be just a person's peculiar ideas. When one does receive specific light, he should be happy to walk in it alone and not try to make others live up to it.

General light has been defined as light that every child of God must have and must walk in if he would build a real Christian character. In disbursing general light, the Holy Ghost uses man as well as the Bible and a godly life as well as the spoken word. To have fellowship with God, one must walk in every ray of general light that comes to him, no matter what kind of a conductor conveys it.

To fellowship him in every sense of the word, one must walk in the light as he is in the light, or in other words, one must live by his standard. Consider now what it means to walk in the fellowship of his light.

It Is Not the Light of Reason

When one walks in his light, he never questions, "Why?" He is not even concerned as to whether he will ever understand the reason, either in this life or the next. The fact that he commands it is enough. If he commands it, there is no hesitancy. To know his will is to obey. To walk in the light as he is in the light means that one never even desires, much less ever asks, him to alter his demands. Ten minutes of obedience will clear up more questions than a lifetime of reasoning. The reason so many people get into spiritual fog is because they refuse to walk in the light. Disobedience in anything will stop the process of God in one's life. Refusal to walk in the light will clothe the soul in darkness, and Jesus said, "How great is that darkness?"

It Is Not the Light of Conscience

Conscience cannot give light. It can only bring condemnation when it is crossed. Light goes ahead of action. Conscience follows it. Light says, "This is the way; walk ye in it." When light is sidestepped, conscience comes in and says, "You have missed the way."

So many people today live by conscience alone. They never place themselves in God's light; therefore, conscience never troubles them and, because it does not, they think they are all right. All kinds of atrocities can be committed by men who live outside the realm of God's light without any compunction of conscience. Conscience outside of God's light is not only an unsafe guide, it is not even a safe judge.

It Is Not the Light of Jewish Law

There are three great codes of law mentioned in the Old Testament: the ceremonial code, the Jewish national code and the moral code. The ceremonial code was fulfilled in Jesus Christ and became inoperative when he died. The Jewish national code was given for the Jews as a nation alone, so when the nation ceased to exist as such, the laws were of no further use. The moral code was given for the world for all time and, therefore, is still in force.

The moral code is covered by the Ten Commandments. Every statement in the moral code has been restated in the New Testament and is, therefore, obligatory upon all people now. However, that is not the light for this day. In the restatement of the law Jesus went a little further than Moses. Read in Matthew 5:27, "Ye have heard that it was said by them of old time, Thou shalt not commit adultery: But I say unto you, that whosoever looketh on a women to lust after her hath committed adultery with her already in his heart." The law said, "Thou shalt love the Lord thy God with all thy heart, and with all thy soul, and with all thy strength, and with all thy mind; and thy neighbor as thyself." But Jesus said, "A new commandment I give unto you, that ye love one another as I have loved you." It is true that holiness thundered in the law, but all the light of the law could do was to reveal the need of holiness. If one walks in the light of Jesus Christ, his light enables one to obtain holiness. "But if we walk in the light, as he is in the light, we have fellowship one with another, and the blood of Jesus Christ his Son cleanseth us from all sin."

It Is Walking According to His Standards

It is walking according to his standards relative to the new birth. He said, "Except a man be born again he cannot see the Kingdom of God." He did not say "may not," but "cannot." "Except your righteousness shall exceed the righteousness of the scribes and Pharisees, ye shall in no case enter into the kingdom of heaven." Their righteousness was made up of outward forms and liturgical ceremonies. To live by his standard, one must have more than outward form. He must have more than morality touched by emotion. He must have more than development. The new birth is not a question of development, but of generation. It is not human effort, but a divine birth (John 3:3). It is a gift of divine power (John 1:12). It brings a divine indwelling (Galatians 4:6). It brings a revelation of divine characteristics and not just an improvement of human characteristics.

It is living by his standard relative to heart purity. If one walks in his light, he said that his blood would cleanse from all sin. It is not by growth. One is either cleansed or not cleansed. If one is walking in his light, he has been made pure even as he is pure. The devil can come and look one over and still that one can say with Jesus, "The prince of this world cometh and hath nothing in me." Even God can look one over and find nothing in him to condemn. Enoch lived there, and it is written, "He pleased God." When one lives there today, all he is, does, thinks or says will be pleasing in God's sight.

It is here one lives in his light relative to obedience to the will of God. He said, "I came down from heaven, not to do mine own will, but the will of him that sent me." The Psalmist declared, "I delight to do thy will." It is here we become identified with him. It is here he lives in one, and one lives in him. Here a man is close enough to hear his voice, yea, close enough to feel the pulsation of the desires of his heart and to feel the gentle checking of his Spirit. If one fails to obey the gentle check of the Spirit, at once shadows are thrown across his path, spiritual fog enshrouds the soul, and the music of the dove of peace is silenced in the heart while the dove perches to take its flight. Continue to disobey the checks of the Spirit, and soon the shadows turn to darkness and the song of the dove of peace will be exchanged for the croaking of the raven of despair.

A person in such a condition may still profess religion, but dry rot has taken the place of perennial freshness in his spiritual life. He is continually harking back to the experiences of other days. He tries to patch present disobedience with past victories. While he lived in the light of Christ, he took a stand against anything and everything that he thought might grieve him. Now he sympathizes with it and makes excuses for it. He is usually hard in his heart, harsh in his spirit, critical of the present while he lives in the past. Such people are sometimes more defiant than devout. Many times they substitute argument for abandonment. All of this had come because somewhere they murdered the checks of the Spirit and failed to walk in the light.

How is it with you, dear reader? Are you bringing up the bottom of your life to the top of your light? Are you living up to the standards you think others should live by? Are you obeying quickly what he reveals to you in secret? Have you confronted with his light the hidden recesses of your heart? Are you honest with God and man? Are you sure you are not walking in craftiness or handling the Word of God deceitfully? When that crisis came and God asked you to go beyond others, did you refuse for fear of criticism? Can you look God and man in the face and honestly declare you are walking in his light as found in I Corinthians 13? Are you walking in his light relative to the things of the material world, the love of the world, your own accomplishments, your attitudes toward your friends, your relatives and your enemies? Is your prayer life, your Bible study, your compassion for souls and your giving according to his light? Are you living in his light in relation to the judgment? Are you fearful of the judgment or his coming?

Reader, if you live in his light here, then you can look forward to the judgment with joy and delight. You will know that anything wrong the judgment might reveal has already been revealed and rectified. All the judgment will reveal will be the mighty working of grace in your heart and life. In Ephesians 2:1 it says, "And you hath he quickened, who were dead in trespasses and sins." Then drop down to the seventh verse and read, "That in the ages to come he might shew the exceeding riches of his grace in his kindness towards us through Christ Jesus." Amen and Amen!

14

Christian Delinquency

WE ARE HEARING MUCH in these days about juvenile delinquency, and some say it is the result of parental delinquency. But may not both juvenile and parental delinquency be charged to Christian delinquency? To the early church, Christian character meant more than it does today. If we study Christian character as it is revealed in the inspired standard and contrast it with what appears in the actual life of professed Christians today, we will be astonished at the dissimilarity.

Read of Christian character as it is sketched in the life of Jesus Christ, who is its author and pattern. See how far we are from that pattern. Look at it as it is depicted in the Sermon on the Mount and the theology of Paul. Look at it as it manifests itself in the Acts of the Apostles and radiates from the Philippian church. There we have our standard for Christian character. And we are Christian only insofar as we conform to the standard. There seems to be a world of difference between what Christian character should be and what it really is; and when we contrast them, we must conclude there is much Christian delinquency. We want to notice here some ways in which professed Christians are delinquent.

Religion, A Secondary Consideration

God's business is the chief business of every Christian. We can learn this from our Leader. One of his first revealed utterances is, "Wist ye not that I must be about my Father's business?" He instructed his followers to seek first the kingdom of God and his righteousness. They get it also from the great Christian leader Paul. He said, "This one thing I do, forgetting those things which are behind…, I press toward the mark for the prize of the high calling of God in Christ Jesus." His one business and aim was religion.

If our religion is anything at all, it should be everything to us. How few, comparatively speaking, of professed Christians make their religion "all and in all." Self-interest and the concerns of earth take first place in so many lives. Few can say with Paul, "For me to live is Christ." This is not criticism, for do we not all know that the majority of professed Christians make the interest of God's kingdom, the spread of the gospel, and the salvation of man a secondary concern? Their manner of living tells the world that their farms, businesses, jobs, professions, homes, friendships, bank accounts, and pleasures take first place in their thinking, desires, and activities. All the infidels on earth, and all the modernistic preachers in the pulpits, and all the saloons on street corners cannot do more to retard the work of God than a church filled with such self-seeking professors of religion.

Fickleness

Religion should be a lifelong habit. It was so with David and Daniel. It was so with Paul and Jesus Christ. Paul said, "Be ye steadfast, unmoveable, always abounding in the work of the Lord." Strength in anything is gained by systematic, consistent effort. The laws by which Christian character is built are not capricious or sudden in their operation. Fickleness in religion greatly hinders the individual controlled by it. Those who are fickle come to the place where they lose confidence in other men, in God, and in themselves. They will then either live in a world of giddiness without concern or of fear without foundation. Their religion is periodical and spasmodic. They finally become a human chameleon. Their sinning or saintliness is determined by crowds or condition. Their praying is determined by necessity or prosperity. Their religion is hot or cold according to revivals or reverses. The tragedy is that such people will eventually drift with the crowd and be lost forever.

Lack of Love

Ever since the inception of the Christian church, there has been a tendency to substitute. There has been a substitution of refinement for regeneration, of attainment for the atonement, of education for the enduement of power, and of labor for love. There seems to be so much will worship today; it moves the hands, the feet, and the lips in service, but it is not impelled by love. We need more of that spirit that cries out, "The love of Christ constraineth us."

"God is love." Jesus Christ was love incarnate. Love made him leave the splendor of heaven, prompted all of his activities, and led him to Calvary. His dying expressions were expressions of love. "Woman, behold thy son!" To John he said, "Behold, thy mother!" "Father, forgive them; for they know not what they do." His resurrection acts and expressions were prompted by love. The angel, in bearing the Savior's message, said, "Go tell his disciples and Peter." What love is here expressed! Jesus himself said, "Go ye into all the world and preach the Gospel to every creature." In the estimation of this writer, this statement packs into a few words more love than any statement ever uttered by God or man. Nothing but love would have impelled his disciples to carry on his labors, suffer the marks of crucifixion in their bodies, and finally become martyrs to his cause.

What is religion without an impelling, compelling, undying, self-denying love?

> Though I speak with the tongues of men and of angels, and have not charity, I am become as sounding brass or a tinkling symbol. And though I have the gift of prophecy, and understand all mysteries, and all knowledge; and though I have all faith so that I could remove mountains, and have not charity, I am nothing. And though I bestow all my goods to feed the poor, and though I give my body to be burned, and have not charity, I am nothing.

We certainly see by this that without love all religion is vanity. It is distressing to contrast Jesus' love for God and man and the love of his great apostle Paul for God and man with the anemic, loveless, superficial religion of today. Paramount unbrotherliness, petty quarrels, jealousies between denominations, envies between leaders, evil speaking between most all professors of religion, and uncharitableness between ministers contrast very unfavorably with Jesus' evidence of true Christianity when he said, "By this shall all men know that ye are my disciples, if ye have love one to another."

15

More Signs of Christian Delinquency

IN THE LAST CHAPTER we raised the question as to whether or not juvenile delinquency could be attributed to parental delinquency and whether both could not be traced back to Christian delinquency. In that chapter we cited some signs of Christian delinquency. There are a few more to which we should like to call attention here.

Lack of Personal Holiness

If a man seeks any religion at all from Jesus Christ, he seeks a holy religion. Christ provides no other kind. His words that have been written down for us portray a religion that is holy. They wage relentless warfare against sin. They reveal the malignancy of sin by the eternal principles of truth. His Word depicts a hatred of sin and tells of an eternal hell as punishment for its devotees. Read it if you doubt this.

The Scriptures, speaking of Christ, say he "did no sin, neither was guile found in his mouth." He could say of himself, "The prince of this world cometh, and hath nothing in me." He said to his disciples, "Blessed are the pure in heart;" and, "Be ye therefore perfect, even as your Father which is in heaven is perfect." The Apostle Paul declared, "Follow peace with all men, and holiness, without which no man shall see the Lord." The Apostle Peter picked out from the Old Testament and placed in the New the statement, "Be ye holy; for I am holy." Jesus' precepts and those of his disciples demand holiness of heart, holiness of life, and holiness of thought. They demand holiness in the church life, holiness in one's private life, holiness in one's home life, and holiness in one's public life. Holiness is required in social life as well as in business relationships. When we consider this, how short do we come? How unscriptural are the lives of most professors?

What a vast difference there is in the Christian religion as written in the Scriptures and that which is exemplified in the actions of many who profess it! There are far too many people identifying themselves with Christianity and affiliating themselves with the church who crave from these associations too little influence in their character or on their conduct. Too often neither their tempers or tongues are controlled. They are lax in morals and Sunday observance, in common honesty, and careless in handling the truth. They are engrossed in material gain, overreaching in business transactions, uncharitable in their demands for charity from others. Too often they are revengeful toward those who have wronged them—outwardly appeasing, yet inwardly unforgiving. There are too many who are haughty toward inferiors and stinted in their giving to God's work.

A lack of holiness in the ranks of the professed holy is the cause of much of our failure with God and man. It is not so much holiness the world is opposing, but the lack of it. The quantity of religion in our churches without quality is a grief to God and a disgust to man. Inconsistencies in professors produce an indifference in sinners. Sinners feel safe when sinning saints profess they are saved. If the holiness movement is ever to see a great revival, she must return to radical, practical holiness. We can not impress the world with the importance of our religion unless we are imitators of its Founder.

Lack of Humility

Humility is almost a lost virtue. It is, however, an essential in the religion of Christ. "God resisteth the proud, but giveth grace to the humble." And again, "He that humbleth himself shall be exalted." Its Founder humbled himself as no other being could ever do. "He humbled himself, and became obedient unto death, even the death of the cross." He said, "Come unto me, all ye that labor and are heavy laden, and I will give you rest. Take my yoke upon you, and learn of me; for I am meek and lowly in heart; and ye shall find rest unto your souls." He was born in humility, lived in humility, sought humble companionship, and died a humiliating death.

Humility is the core of the Christian religion. It is an essential part of it. It is not only the center of it, but it is the outer garment. "Be clothed with humility." How little of it is manifest, but how much of its opposite, pride, is in evidence. Men are proud of their face, their place, their grace, their force, their genealogy, their wealth, their talents (both natural and acquired), and their social position. Some workers in the church so far forget their source of power that they are puffed up over their preaching, their singing, their praying, and their teaching ability. How many men exalt themselves when they give more to the cause of God than others! Such Christian delinquency is a disgust to the world. They want none of it. It is a contributing factor to sinking the world deeper into the ditch of godlessness.

Buoyancy of Spirit

A joyless Christian is a weakling. "The joy of the Lord is your strength." The Gospel is called "good tidings of great joy, which shall be to all people." The truth of salvation is the most blissful tiding in the universe. Its whole purpose is to remove from the heart of man that which brings woe and heartache. It delivers men from all their troubles because it gives him the Burden Bearer. Paul exhorts his people to cast "all your care upon him; for he careth for you." The salvation of Jesus delivers from melancholy and produces a heaven on earth in heart and home.

It brings a contentment that cannot be described. It enables one to cry, "I have learned in whatsoever state I am, therewith to be content." It makes people happy, even in the house of their bondage. They can sing in the prison, as Paul and Silas and even as Madam Guyon. It lifts one up and takes his feet out of the miry clay, placing them upon the solid rock and puts a new song in his mouth, even praises unto God. It gives joy in tribulation, peace in war, and calm in storm. It was so in Israel's day. Israel was exhorted to sing for joy (Isaiah 65:14). Israel, we are told, shouted for joy (Ezra 3:12). They offered sacrifices of joy (Psalm 27:6). They had a joyful religion, even back under the law. It was so also in the days of Jesus Christ. He said, "Blessed are ye, when men shall revile you and persecute you, and shall say all manner of evil against you falsely, for my sake. Rejoice, and be exceeding glad: for great is your reward in heaven."

Joy possessed the hearts of God's people in the early days of the reformation under the Wesleys and the revival of the early days of our own land. It was especially so at the birth of the present-day holiness movement. That joyful spirit attracted thousands of people to the ranks of holiness who would never have been drawn there simply by the theology of the holiness people. Today it seems too conspicuous by its absence.

Intellectualism, formality, and funeral piety have taken its place. Men have turned from it because of the inconsistencies in the lives of those who have seemed to be emotional in their religion. Today it is said that shouting is only the indication of a shallow mind trying to express itself and that intelligent people never give vent to their feeling. What an insult to the Christ who said, "If these should hold their peace, the stones would immediately cry out;" and to Paul who said, "Rejoice in the Lord always: and again I say, Rejoice." I am not pleading for excesses in demonstration, but I do plead for that joy that gives strength, that manifestation of it that is an attraction to the world, without which any church will have empty pews and barren altars.

16

The Progress and Product of Christian Missions

IT HAS BEEN A pleasure to labor with missionaries from the Oriental Missionary Society, World Gospel Mission and our own missionaries from the Pilgrim missionary work. I have enjoyed their fellowship and deeply enjoyed their messages. I want them to know that I deeply appreciate what they are doing to get this gospel out to the lost of the earth. After all, we are not trying to build denominations; we are trying to build the kingdom of God and win souls for Jesus Christ.

The theme of this convention has been witnessing and I have finally caught up with the theme of the convention. If you will study the New Testament, you will find this was the method Christ used and Christ ordained from the beginning to get his gospel to the ends of the earth. But in this lecture I am noticing how far the church drifted from his purpose and from his plan. I am noticing in this lecture the progress and product of Christian missions. I would like to divide this into several missionary periods and note the difference in the progress in each period.

First, the Apostolic Period. This period must ever stand in a class by itself. The nearness to the days of Christ on earth and the spark given to it by those men who had been with him will always make this period unique. It was unique in its extension. One gospel tells us, "They went everywhere preaching the Word," from Jerusalem to Persia, Arabia, Mesopotamia, Asia Minor, Greece, Italy, Egypt and other parts of North Africa. It had been taken to these countries by the apostles themselves.

Second, the Early Church Period. During the next generation the borders in the church were extended, not by a few leaders or an extensive organized movement, but by men witnessing. The entire church was so endued with the spirit of witness that the gospel spread through such channels as ordinary social intercourse, commerce and travel. Every Christian was a herald of the Gospel. Its growth was so rapid in that period that Justin Martyr, who lived in the years from 103 to 165, said:

> There is no people, Greek or Barbarian or any other race, by whatsoever manner they may be distinguished of art or agriculture, whether they dwell in tents or wander about in covered wagons, among whom prayers and thanksgivings are not offered in the name of the Crucified Jesus.

Tertullian said, "We are but of yesterday and yet we already fill your cities, your islands, your camps, your palaces, your senate, your forum; we have left you only your temples." Origen, who lived from A.D. 185 to 251, said:

> I'm now considering how in a few years and with no great store of teachers in spite of the attacks which would cost us life and property, the preaching of that Word has found its way into every part of the world, so that Greeks and Barbarians, wise and unwise, adhere to the religion of Jesus.

Eusebius, who lived from A.D. 166 to 240, said:

> There flourished at that time many successors of the apostles who reared the edifice on foundations which they laid. Continuing the work of the preaching of the Gospel and scattering abundantly over the whole earth the wholesome seed of the heavenly kingdom for a very large number of disciples carried away by fervent love of the truth which the divine Word revealed unto them fulfill the command of the Savior to divide their goods among the poor, then taking leave of their country, they filled the office of evangelists coveting eagerly to spread Christ and to carry the glad tidings of God to those who had not heard the word of faith. And after laying the foundations of the faith in some remote and barbarous countries, establishing pastors among them and confiding to them the care of those young settlements without stopping longer they hastened on to other nations attended by the grace and virtue of God.

While it is impossible to give accurate statements of the number of Christians at the close of this period, estimates of authorities range from one-tenth to one-twentieth of the entire population of the Roman Empire. By the opening of the fourth century, Christianity had so covered the then known world and its intellectual moral power had created such an influence, it could not be ignored. It must be dealt with. State rulers regarded its adherents with suspicion, lest it should weaken the imperial grasp on great provinces. The state prohibited the faith and persecution set in. Ten distinct persecutions are recorded, ranging from 264 under Nero to 303. Under Nero they were burned at the stake to serve as nocturnal lights, nailed to crosses and covered with skins of wild animals to be worried to death by dogs. In the catacombs of St. Sebastian alone are the bones of 174,000 martyrs. This persecution did not extinguish—it only fanned the flame. The blood of the martyrs proved then, as it must prove now, to be the seed of the church. The growth of the church during this period was perhaps the greatest of any time in the history of the church.

Third, early European History. I am noticing the drift from this early period. At this time Constantine came to power and found he could not stamp out Christianity, so he deferred to it, making it the religion of the state. All students of history know the story of his covenant—his seeing a cross in the sky with the words, "By this sign, conquer," and adopting it as the standard for his armies. Persecution from without caused the church to grow; having ceased, opposition from within almost gave it its deathblow.

Simplicity of worship gave way to the liturgical worship which took over the spiritual. Spiritual declension set in. Missionary zeal began to wane. National conversion instead of individual conversion took over, producing the curse of Jesuit missions and making the church an easy prey for Mohammedanism. Theological controversies set in and the missionary vision was blurred.

Monasticism was the result and for but a few heroic souls—like the one nicknamed the Little Wolf, missionary to the Goths, or Martin, missionary to the Gauls or French, and Patrick the missionary to Ireland, and Columbo, the missionary to Scotland, Augustine, the missionary to England, or Columbanis, the missionary to Germany, and others—there was little missionary work done. The kind that was done was mostly forcing the masses to adopt religion rather than converting the individual by the power of the Gospel. It was during this period that Mohammedanism spread rapidly over the Middle East by force. Even until this day it is held in the iron embrace of the Christless religion.

Fourth, the Period of the Middle Ages. Little good can be said for the church of this age. It produced some noble souls. The growth of the church, meaning the Catholic church, was either by pomp and ceremony which always has and, even to our day, appealed to the heathen unlearned and shallow and to the small souls only by force. It has conversions to the church, but not as individuals to Jesus Christ, and I am afraid that much of that is creeping into the Protestant church today. It was the day of the crusades which did much more harm than good. Their history is so dark I do not like to read it and do not like to repeat it. Through the orders of Jesus or the Jesuits, the church, not the Gospel, was taken to India, Japan, the Philippines, Africa, South America, Mexico and Canada. With but few exceptions in the period, missionary endeavors cursed the world more than it blessed it, and the curse still hangs as a pall over the nations then reached.

Fifth, the Period of the Reformation. This period was not missionary in character. It was a battle against Ecclesiastical abuses and corruption within the church. The leaders within the Reformation seemed to have no serious sense of their obligation to evangelize the unreached of earth. In this age we have the spectacle of the corrupt church carrying on to some extent enthusiastically a missionary work, while the Protestant church cared nothing for missions.

This fact is hard to understand. It should, however, point up to us the great danger of a wrong emphasis. The church had failed to obey the great commission. The voice of the pulpit was silenced on it. The ministry was enthralled on theological controversy, which was bringing death to the church as it will ever do. The most important mission of the church was neglected. Had it not been for the Pietist movement being born at this time, lifting up a standard of holy living and putting an emphasis on missionary responsibility, Protestantism could have died soon after its birth.

It took a layman to awaken a dying church. He propounded in writing just three questions on missions. First, is it right that we evangelical Christians hold the Gospel ourselves alone? Second, is it right for the church to have so many theological students and the most of them labor at home while we do little to induce them to labor abroad? Third, is it right that we spend so much on clothing, eating, drinking and the many delicacies and have hitherto thought of no means for the spread of the Gospel of Jesus Christ?

These questions, instead of awakening the church or clergy, brought the wrath of both on his head until he fled to Holland and from there to Dutch Guinea, where he died for the cause of missions; but not in vain, for what his writings could not do, his death did do. The controversy over the great truth of justification by faith caused church leaders to neglect the glorious truth of entire sanctification and, by doing so, caused corruption to set in in the newly formed Protestant church. This gave birth to the Pietist movement, which in turn gave birth in 1698 to a university which was the birthplace of the first organized missionary effort. This movement was led by Philip Spencer, the John Wesley of Germany. From this school missionaries went to India. Other like colleges began to spring into being, and from these trained missionaries were sent to other countries.

From the Pietist movement the Moravians received their missionary call. While Luther is known as the Father of the Reformation, Pietist societies existed before he nailed his thesis to the door of Wittenberg. At the time of the Awakening of the Reformation, Pietists are known to have as high as four hundred organized churches. They suffered greatly under the hand of the Jesuits until they were almost exterminated when they met Count Zinzendorf, who not only gave them refuge but financial aid and perhaps saved them from extermination. Zinzendorf and his consecrated wife not only gave themselves to God, but they gave all of their earthly possessions. In 1734 he had his first great awakening on foreign missions, and from that time on enabled the Moravian Church to become such a missionary church that no church or missionary movement in our day has ever approached it in missionary devotion.

We are now in what is perhaps the last stage to the missionary endeavor. This is the sixth one. It is known as the period of Modern Missions. The age was started when William Carey preached a sermon in the Baptist church. (God bless the Baptists.) His two main points were: "Expect much from God and undertake great things for God." Although he never said so in words, he lived by the theory that whatsoever one undertakes for God, God will underwrite. At the close of that message, a number of Baptist ministers met and organized the first modern missionary society.

Carey was responsible for changing missionary effort from the individualistic to the organizational. From that date, 1792, missionary endeavor has gone both backward and forward. It has gone back to the Pentecostal church and to the missionary days of Paul for both inspiration and methods. It will never die until he comes who said: "Occupy till I come." We are possibly witnessing the last great effort to get the gospel to the world before he comes. Frantically, men look for the best methods through which to accomplish the task. What are some?

I have time to notice only one. I will note two phases, or perhaps three phases, of it. I believe in medical missions and encourage them, for I know their value, firsthand. I believe in the day-school method and encourage it, as I have seen it work successfully. I believe in the colporteur method and have seen it work and back it up fully, for it certainly works in getting out the Gospel. To me, however, the greatest method is that of the early church. And the method of the early church was *evangelism*. Evangelize, evangelize, evangelize was their watchword. This is the heart of the missionary work and must be kept uppermost in it.

I note it in its three phases. First, the printed page, and I wish some would take journalism and get into missionary work along that line and create some literature for our missionary work. You could not serve your generation better than in that field. Then mass evangelism. The evangelist who is going to engage in mass evangelism in foreign lands must know the people among whom he is laboring. He must know their history and background. He must know their customs. He must know their way of thinking. He must know their religion. He must have a knowledge and a great knowledge of the Word of God. He must be genuine in his experience of saving grace and he must have the fullness of the blessing of holiness. Some people are asking to take evangelistic trips. Personally, I do not advise everyone to go to foreign fields on evangelistic trips, for, unless you line up and know and measure up to what I have just given, your ministry in mass evangelism in foreign countries will certainly be limited.

Personal evangelism. This was and is for the layman. After the Day of Pentecost the early church went from house to house publishing the Gospel. There are two great "shalls" in the statements of Jesus I cannot get away from. "But ye shall receive power after that the Holy Ghost is come upon you." You have never seen in your life a powerless, sanctified person. Every person who is filled with the Holy Ghost, the Scripture says, has power; power for what?

"Ye shall be witnesses unto me." So we have power not to sit around in our churches and dissipate that power given to us by the Holy Ghost by doing nothing for a world that is rushing on toward hell past our doors, that we hardly have any effect on at all, and they hardly know that we are in existence. But when the Holy Ghost comes into your heart, he will give you power to witness. The early church was a witnessing church. In the first few years of its existence 50,000 souls were won in Jerusalem alone or in Palestine, I should say, not by preachers, not by apostles, but by the witness of the laymen. For two hundred years it remained a witnessing church. After two hundred years the laymen who had carried the witnessing tried to push it off on the minister. When they did, the church began to die and soon was in the dark ages.

If we are going to save the Christian church today at home and abroad, we must have laymen filled with the Holy Ghost, laymen so filled with the Holy Ghost they will become witnesses and carry this gospel message out to their own kind in their own land. It was the method of Jesus Christ. He has never reversed or revoked his method. It is still the method he would like for his church to use. Does it work? I think it does.

Allow me to close this lecture on a little different plane, will you, noticing the power of witnessing. When I was in Mexico, the last conference I attended there, I could not preside. I was a foreigner; Rev. Soltero was presiding. A man sixty-five years of age arose and said, "May I give my report to this conference?" Brother Soltero said, "Proceed, Sir." He said, "I'm 65 years of age. I am not a preacher; I am a layman. I work every day for my livelihood, but after I've labored all day, I go from hut to hut and house to house, telling people about Jesus Christ. And in the last twelve months, by going from house to house, talking about Jesus and witnessing, I have won 46 people to Jesus Christ." I say, witnessing has a power about it when one is filled with the Holy Ghost that even preaching does not have.

I think of being on the island of Jamaica with Brother Phillippe's brother. He was in charge of the work on the island at that time. He rented the Ward Theater. We were having as high as two thousand to preach to nightly and turning away as high as eight hundred a night. In one service during the campaign a young lady came to the alter. She came back the second night. She came back the third night, and the third night she was gloriously sanctified. She was a nurse in the city hospital in Kingston. When I returned to Jamaica three years later, holding another meeting, I received a letter from that nurse. She said: "Dear Brother Flexon, I'm sorry I cannot attend your services this year; I'm on night duty. In the last three years since God has filled me with the Holy Spirit, I have won thirty-six nurses to Jesus Christ in this hospital by my personal testimony."

I am talking about the power of witnessing. This convention had as its theme *witnessing*. What we need today, at home and abroad, is more laymen filled with the Holy Spirit who will go out and witness. I think of being in Africa. After a Sunday camp meeting service, I went out to visit villages on Monday. I met the older people, and as I met them, I said, "I did not see you at camp meeting yesterday. Why didn't you attend the camp meeting?" They said, "You've come too late for us. We're so steeped in our superstition, our lives are so dark we can't understand what you say. Get our children; get our young people. We want them to be Christians, but you've come too late for us."

As I walked from these villages, I wondered how I would feel when I meet those people at the judgment bar of God and God would say to them, "Depart from me, you workers of iniquity; I never knew you," and they look over at me and say, "You came too late for us." I wonder how many more are going to have to say that the missionary has come too late.

I think this morning of Bill Thomas, preaching on the island of Indianoo. He was preaching on heaven. He was preaching about the glories of heaven and the blessing that we are going to enjoy in heaven. And, finally, he came to the thought that one thing that is going to make heaven besides the presence of Jesus Christ will be to meet your loved ones when you get to heaven. They had been "amening" him up until that time, but when he made that statement, they dropped their heads. There were no more "amens" and the tears started down their faces.

Brother Thomas did not know what to make of it, but after the service he said, "You were 'amening' me until I came to the thought that you would enjoy meeting your loved ones, your fathers and mothers who have gone on before you, when you get to heaven. Then you stopped 'amening' and dropped your heads and began to weep. What made you do it?" They said, "Because we'll not meet them there, for no one ever came to tell them what you are telling us and they died without ever hearing."

How many more are going to have to die without hearing because we want other things rather than the will of God for our lives?

17

The Plan of Salvation for the Unreached

I DO NOT WISH to seem to be like a dark man going down a dark cellar with a dark lantern looking after a dark cat, for I am not a pessimist but a realist. I never have been afraid to face up to facts, and that is exactly what I want to do today. After being in missionary work twenty-three years, giving the best of my life to it, serving eleven years as assistant to the secretary of foreign missions, one year as field superintendent over our work in the West Indies, and twelve years as secretary of foreign missions of our church, I am convinced that we are not making it. We are not getting the job done I feel God would have us to do. And I say this generally speaking, not only for one denomination, but for the Protestant church in general.

After 150 years of missionary work in India, what kind of a picture do we have? Or possibly after one hundred years of missionary work in Korea, what do we have to show for it? You say, "Much," and I agree with that; but, nevertheless, I wonder if we are getting the job done. The modern missionary movement began in 1792 when the Baptist Society for the Promotion of the Gospel organized after a sermon on missions by William Cary. Since then, every country has to some degree had a gospel message of some kind. Some of these people have accepted; the vast majority have rejected.

The following statistics are the most up-to-date statistics I could find. There is a total of 888,803,000 people in the world today who bear the name of "Christian." 527,136,000 are Roman Catholics. 137,136,000 are Eastern Orthodox. 214,133,000 are Protestants. There are 12,335,000 Jews, 430,205,000 Moslems, 300,920,000 Confucianists, 150,910,000 Buddhists, 322,170,000 Hindus, 121,150,000 primitive people and 524,000,000 plus with no religion at all. Many more that have not been counted are still unreached by the gospel. But

214,000,000 it seems to me is a very small percent out of nearly three billion people. To be in the Protestant ranks, the question that rises is, what part of the task yet remains to be accomplished?

Besides the picture given above, I quote from Oswald Smith, "There are at least 2,974 major languages spoken by man." At the present time 1,789 of them have never had one word of the gospel messages written to them. This means only 1,185 have the gospel message reduced to writing. This is staggering and most maddening to one who loves Jesus Christ. There are over 1,000 tribes without any gospel at all, either written or oral.

The church knows where they are. Three hundred fifty of them are in Africa, three hundred are in South America. One hundred of them are in India. Seventy-five are in Siberia, dark Siberia with no one to tell of drudgeries and darkness; one hundred seventy-five tribes in China, Indo-China and the Philippines; in Brazil alone more than 5,000,000 Indians who have never once heard; in Bolivia 100,000 pure-blooded Indians; in Peru 2,500,000 Indians. In Columbia there are 100,000 low-land Indians, most of them in savage, primitive conditions and 500,000 highland Indians mostly in only a semi-civilized state.

If we believe what we preach—and we should believe it or stop preaching it, that only those that are born again will see the kingdom of God and only those that are pure in heart will see God—then we must conclude that ninety percent of the population of the world does not yet understand anything about the power of the blood of Jesus Christ to save men from all sin. I am stepping in new territory in this lecture. I am sticking my neck out a long ways. I may be heckled at, but it will not be the first time, and I may not see accomplished in my lifetime what I propose; but if I can drop a seed that will lodge in the mind and the heart of some who are to be future missionaries, I will be satisfied.

I have pointed out the greatness of the task yet ahead of the church in its effort to give the gospel to every creature and to make disciples of all nations. I wish to differentiate between remote unreached areas of earth and the areas unevangelized near to already established mission stations. I am noticing in this lecture the plan for reaching both of these areas, for both as yet are unaffected by the gospel.

One could wish for a more comprehensive united plan of action on the part of all churches and missionary societies in our effort to reach the goal set by Jesus Christ. Such a plan might well lead to the established mission stations and the evangelization of the areas adjacent to them, the weaker societies in a workable agreement so that all men might have one chance to at least hear them. This would save the confusion by societies trampling on each other's toes in an effort to propagate a denominati nal emphasis. In such a workable agreement the areas adjacent to the already well-organized and well-established mission stations might well be at least evangelized in our generation. The evangelization of and the making of disciples in the more remote areas would then be accomplished by assigning such areas to new societies created for that purpose.

You may say this plan will not work. It will not work, you say, for several reasons. I might call attention to some of them that you might propose. First, the smaller societies would be swallowed up in the larger societies and lose their field and their constituency. That need not be. If man can just agree on the policy that they wish to adopt, they will somehow find a way to carry it out and find some method by which to accomplish it.

Second, you say men must be called to labor in certain areas of mission life, and they must labor always where called. That can hardly be substantiated. First, because men may mistake the place of the call. I have known young people who said they had a call to fields that were closed to all missionary endeavor by American missionaries. But they refused to go elsewhere. Therefore, their missionary call was never consummated or climaxed. Some such fields have been closed for years. And, as far as we know, may never open again. I realize God knows the future; we do not. He may see the doors will open again to that particular field and, therefore, call for recruits. However, I know of some who have waited for doors to open to a certain field for the past fifteen years and they are growing old and they are waiting while the doors are locked against them; but they refuse to go elsewhere. I hope you that are called to mission lands will never get in that condition.

Some of the most successful missionaries of all times have been those who said they were called to a certain field and, when the doors where closed to them in that particular field and the doors opened to another field, they entered them and the world and heaven will ever be richer because of their dedication to a Person and his cause and not just to a field. T. C. Studd was one in that class, his call being to China. The

Boxer Rebellion closed the door to that field. The door to Africa opened and he entered. Because he did, his name will always adorn the walls of Africa's dedicated missionaries.

Second, because a call to be a missionary is for all times, as far as we are concerned, and for all the world. The missionary heart that does not embrace the world needs to be enlarged.

Third, you may say selfish denominational ambitions would prohibit the promulgation and operation for such a plan. That is conceded, if we are to consider all Protestant denominations. But that certainly should not be so among denominations professing holiness of heart. Nothing is more distressing to me than to see those groups which profess the same doctrines and hold to almost the same standards of practice, treading on each other's toes in a frantic effort to build a denomination rather than unite in an effort to build the kingdom of God and get the gospel to the ends of the world.

Returning to the proposition of united, concerted and thoroughly planned effort on the part of all born-again evangelicals, as far as possible, to at least place a portion of the Word of God in the hands of every unreached person and use every resource at their command to evangelize every unevangelized creature, there is little doubt in my mind but that the task would be completed in one generation, and I say that after careful study. For such a plan to be effected, the world field of missions would need to be surveyed and the responsibility of all carefully and authoritatively determined. This would do away with the disasters of overlapping. Creative effort would be made by all to rise to the challenge of new and greater responsibilities, and the work of world evangelism would move forward faster.

Too much missionary work has been done in patches. Too often the patches have been in large cities along the coast. Rural districts and the interior of large countries have been woefully neglected. Then, too, many times when missionary societies have established themselves in cities, they have been too seclusive and have been too satisfied to farm their little patch. There are just too many little patches in some cities fighting to maintain certain denominational distinctives, while the unreached masses perish all around about them. I mean these that are outside the patch present, in many ways, the most pathetic class of heathen on earth.

They are so near to the light, but it never shines on them. In some ways, such as material things, they benefited by being close to the gospel, but never even hear of its power to save man from sin.

This condition, no doubt, exists because of a lack of a definite plan on the part of the individual society or a concerted unified effort on the part of all of the Christians in each of the places. We cannot place the responsibility for this condition on a lack of missionary personnel. In countries where there are the largest concentrations of missionaries this condition remains. It cannot be placed at the door of a shortage of finance, because societies with large financial resources are as guilty as those who live from month-to-month. To say it is because of inadequate facilities with which to work is begging the question. It no doubt can be laid at the door step of either indifference, a lack of vision or lack of planning. I am inclined to believe it is the latter. I would not want to charge missionary societies with indifference or lack of vision, but certainly we have been woefully lacking in all missionary work in the Protestant churches in our planning.

If the already established societies would philosophically devise a plan for evangelizing the areas adjacent to their stations or compounds and would, through such a plan, energetically and with thoroughness press forward to evangelize such areas, and the new societies—and they are springing up constantly—which are coming to birth could, if they would, organize to evangelize the far-flung untouched areas, in another generation there would be a different picture in mission lands than what I have painted to you today. Too much missionary work has been done without rhyme or reason, and certainly without proper perspective.

In perspective, planning the hard places must not be left out. Plans must not be made to only follow the lines of least resistance. To neglect any because of the dangers involved would be bad policy and indicate disloyalty of Jesus Christ. Risk must be accepted as a part in our planning and not be accepted as valid reason for neglecting the hard fields while we take the line of least resistance. It is high time a united effort be made by evangelical missionary societies to attack the seemingly impregnable areas. The risk to be taken and the dangers to be encountered should be a challenge to invade such fortresses of the enemy in our plans and not exclude them because of hardships or suffering.

I am afraid many times that is what missionary societies have done, till the hard places have been passed by. They have been excluded in our planning because of the hardships or the sufferings. Missionary work demands sacrifice, suffering and even death. Proper planning would not eliminate these entirely, but would smooth out the road on which they are found and thus exclude some of them. Many missionaries would have retained their health and in some instances their lives had there been proper planning before moving into such areas. The five men who lost their lives in trying to reach the Aucas is one example.

Nineteen centuries have passed since Christ commanded, "Go ye," and that means every one of you. Speaking to a class, I asked how many in that large class were called to be missionaries, and four hands were raised. What are the rest of you going to do about the great commission of Jesus Christ when he said, "Go ye into all the world and preach the gospel to every creature"? Yet over half of the world's population have never heard of him. Why? Many reasons, but to me the paramount reason is a lack of real planning on the part of evangelicals. We must now crowd into a few short years the work of centuries, but the emergency that is on us is no reason for haste without plan or preparation. Without these we will still go on fighting a losing battle, and the billions will die without ever hearing even once of Jesus Christ.

The greatest need of the missionary world today is literature in the language of the people of which we are working. I was in Chicago a few days ago at the Accrediting Association for Bible colleges. It turned out to be more of a missionary convention than it did a college convention or educational convention. One man spoke on the great need of creative writing and of literature written in such a way that the natives could understand it in the language that the native could get hold of. He pointed out, and I have believed that for many years, that our greatest need is someone who can create literature that can write in such a way that the natives can get hold of it.

We are going out to teach the natives how to read, and the Communists are rushing in giving them something to read. We teach them to read, but give them very little to read. The Communist have found that vacuum and are filling it by spending four times as much to put Communist literature in the hands of those that we win to Christianity and teach in our schools to read than we Protestants are spending to put Protestant literature in their hands. I am talking about this kind of literature, I think put out by the World Gospel Missionary Society, written in the language of the people. Let me ask you, would it not be wise if the holiness movement—if other evangelicals could not join in because of their denominational or doctrinal differences—or one part of it could furnish and produce literature for all of us?

It seems to me there is a great need in the holiness groups for schools furnishing an internship for all outgoing missionaries. I know we have them created by other denominations or independent people, but why must we holiness people leave to other groups the preparation for our missionaries? It seems to me we could help the cause of Jesus Christ through World Missions if the holiness groups would have a clearing house with representation from all holiness groups to clear any group wishing to enter a new field that is a new field to them, thus saving so much of this overlapping.

I have seen the tragedies that come when one holiness church moves into the territory of another holiness church and plants a lighthouse within a few blocks of the one that has been there for years. It seems to me that if we had a world vision and the cause of Jesus Christ at stake rather than our denominational emphasis, this kind of a thing could be stopped in the holiness movement. It may not be stopped in the evangelical world entirely, but it seems to me that we who profess the experience of holiness ought to some way get together and stop this overlapping that brings so much misunderstanding among the natives.

Perhaps, because of the difference in doctrines, it would not be practical for the evangelical missionary societies to work together well. As we look through this plan of missionary endeavor, the roadblocks might be so great we could not hurdle them; but I came back to it and it seems to me there should be no roadblocks in the path of we who love Jesus Christ. Are you asking us to drop our denominational emphasis? Are you asking us to drop our denominational distinctives? No. I am only asking that we get together and form a plan whereby we will stop this spending thousands of dollars and overlapping when out there there are the millions that are dying, never having one ray of gospel light or one crumb of gospel bread. Paul said of his missionary work, he did not build on other men's foundations.

It has been my privilege to open missionary work in nine different places in the world where the gospel of Jesus Christ had never been heard before in the history of the world. Were I younger and physically able, I would be out there now opening new work, but not near the work of any other holiness body. I abhor it, whether it be in the city or the far reaches of the interior.

I feel like I must digress here for the reasons stated. I feel somewhat like the Scotchman who had returned from India after serving there for many years and was giving a missionary address in a large church. He gave the appeal, but no young people answered the appeal. The missionary fell in his tracks and they carried him from the platform. But when he came to, he said, "Where am I? What has happened?" They told him that he fell unconscious on the platform after making his appeal. He said, "Carry me back, carry me back to the platform." They carried him back. He said, "Hold me up," and they stood beside him and held him up. He looked at that crowd of young people and said, "Does Scotland have no more young men to give for India? I'll give my life there."

And I say to you, if the Pilgrim Holiness Church or any other holiness church has no more young people to give to the cause of missions around the world, if not, then some of us who have worn our lives out in this kind of work are still putting our lives on the altar and saying that we will go; it must be done.

I was in South America back among the Partamona Indians. I preached on Sunday night. Sitting in the back of the chapel or school building were a lot of people that I knew did not belong to that village of Paramakatoy. When I finished and the altar call was over, twenty of them came marching down the aisle. They came on the platform and surrounded me. The man that was leading them was their chief, and he began to speak to me in Portuguese. I did not understand Portuguese. They hurried around and found a young man that did. They brought him in, and he interpreted what the chief was saying. He said, "These are my people, my wife and I with eighteen of our people have walked six days to come and hear you speak and to see you. We have heard you speak, and we want that same kind of a story to be told to our people. I come now to ask you, will you go to my village and give my people that same kind of a story?"

He went on with his plea. I had heard many pleas from heathen chiefs around the world, but never one like that, and, finally, with all the English that he knew, he pointed to himself and said, "Me want serve the God." That is all he knew about God. I looked at him, and when he finished I said, "Chief, I'll go to your village tomorrow." Brother Ferryman was there then, flying the plane, and Brother Phillippe and the wife of the chief flew to a village called Arasaul in Brazil. When we arrived, I took some pictures, the people in such a condition I do not dare to show them, not even in my own home.

When I got out of the plane, they all came and shook hands with me. There was a small building nearby. One man took one hand and another man took the other hand and led me to that little building and we went inside. There were three short benches on which three people were sitting. We had a short service. I preached about the Prodigal Son. When I finished, I held up a song book and said, "Have you ever seen a song book?" They shook their heads no. I held up my Bible and said, "Have you ever seen a Bible in your life?" They shook their heads no and I said, "This is a Bible. This is the book of the Living God."

Then I asked them what the building was for. They said, "We build it for church." I said, "Do you have church service here?" They said, "No, there is no one here to tell us of the true God." I said, "What do you use the building for?" They answered, "We come in here Sunday morning, we come in here Sunday night. We come in here night after night and we just sit and sit and sit." I said, "Do you sing?" They answered, "No." "Do you do anything else?" "No, we just come in here and sit and sit and sit." I said, "Why do you come in here and sit like this night after night?" and they said, "We're hoping sometime that someone will come and tell us of the true God." Before I left them, I promised I would send someone or go back myself.

I went back to Paramakatoy and met the chief. I said, "Chief, I'll either send someone to your village to give them the gospel or, you can depend on it, I'll come myself." He packed up his belongings and with his group walked the six days back to his village. I came on home and as I walked into my living room in Indianapolis, Indiana, my wife was standing in the middle of the living room. I told her what had happened before we even sat down and I said, "I told the chief if I could not get someone else to go that you and I would leave our home and we would move into a hut in his village and give his people the gospel of Jesus Christ." I said, "Wife, what about it?" I can see her now as the tears ran down her face as she said, "I'm ready to go to the ends of the earth to give out this gospel message." Did you have to go? No, a young man finally volunteered and is there today, but I am talking about a dedication, I am talking about a consecration. Do you have it?

RESTITUTION 19

"ACCEPT THE LORD, BUT NO REPENTANCE," 18, 19